Adaptation and Decline: stories of aid and diamonds in Africa

Ann Condy

To Andy, the rock in my life

To Douglas, my dear nephew

A Gigliola, cara suocera ed amica per sempre

Cover picture painted by Ann Condy. Title: Ilha de Moçambique: before the storm hits historic slave port

Copyright © June 2025 Ann Condy
All rights reserved.
The Amazon Endure typeface was designed by
2K/DENMARK in 2025.
Template id: ST-414D415A-25-A01
Printed in The United States.
ISBN: 9798286949373

Table of Contents

Introduction 1

Chapter 1: A swamp in Sierra Leone 11

Chapter 2: Guinea - Baptism by fire and the World Bank Debt Tables 18

Chapter 3: Diamonds in the Wild West of Zaire 47

Chapter 4: 'He who rides on the donkey does not know how hot the ground is' (Ghanaian proverb) 71

Chapter 5: Landmines and urban project in Angola 86

Chapter 6: Brazzaville - "We don't know any Andrew Ward" 103

Chapter 7: The dupes of darling Rwanda 128

Chapter 8: Diamond poacher turned gamekeeper – the story of Martyn Marriott 153

Chapter 9: Nigeria – rats, bats and The Aid Show 179

Chapter 10: Government diamond valuation in Sierra Leone... 205

Chapter 11: Ethiopia and tales of NGOs 231

Chapter 12: Daring deeds and scandal in Angola 249

Chapter 13: Independent evaluations are rarely independent 267

Final Chapter: Adaptation and decline 285

Glossary and Acronyms................................... 296

Acknowledgements 308

Questions for Book Clubs................................ 312

Introduction

Why would anyone write about diamonds and international aid in the same story? At first sight, there is a vast gulf between these industries - they might even be considered the antithesis of each other.

Diamonds are a glittery commodity bound up with Western notions of romance, love, wealth, excitement, and a touch of scandal. The diamond industry came up with one of the most successful advertising pitches of all times, 'A diamond is forever', and glamorous American actress and singer Marilyn Monroe performed the iconic song 'Diamonds are a girl's best friend' in the 1953 film Gentlemen Prefer Blondes. Carol Channing, Jo Stafford, Lena Horne, Emmylou Harris, and T Bone Burnett recorded it too.

Aid is more commonly thought of as charities helping the poor, or the United Nations Children's Fund, UNICEF, rattling the collection cans under our noses at Christmas when we are splurging on gifts, and making us feel guilt-ridden in TV advertisements appealing for money to help thirsty, starving, sick children.

When I started writing this book, I would have said that most people consider it is a good thing to give money to help the poor in poorer countries even if the image of doing good has become a little tarnished in recent years. However, as I was finishing it, the United States announced that it was closing its aid agency USAID, which has unleashed a maelstrom of reactions, perhaps allowing closet doubters of aid to come out and express their views more openly. But there are still plenty of key public figures who are arguing that aid is essential and more aid is necessary.

What has prompted me to include both industries in one story is essentially because I believe that the diamond industry has made great efforts to clean up its performance while the aid industry has blemished its own. This is undoubtedly the opposite of what most people might guess to be true, which makes it an intriguing issue. Both industries have adapted for various reasons, and for another set of reasons both are currently in decline.

Aid has become precisely an industry in recent decades, in which massive increases in funding have resulted in adaptation which I regard as negative, eliciting perverse interests and incentives. The many institutions involved – from the so-called donors and their contractees to African governments and consultants – have generally colluded to exaggerate successes and ignore or minimise failures and unintended consequences such as greater corruption. I say generally because there are plenty of individuals and some organisations calling out the lies and cover-ups, but they are either silenced, ignored, or have too little influence to bring about change.

The diamond industry has adapted in a number of ways I consider positive. It has taken significant steps to clean up its modus operandi from as early as the 1970s, although it took a while to move away from the 'Wild West' days of the diamond cartel, De Beers, exploiting the ignorance of local people. A few key individuals acted as poacher turned gamekeeper and, to borrow a term from the aid industry, these gamekeepers 'empowered' African governments by providing them with the expertise to value and market diamonds and to become joint partners with mining companies. There has been the potential for African governments to gain substantial revenue through diamonds, but realising this potential has depended on whether African leaders were more interested in the profits going to line their own pockets or being used to benefit their citizens.

The industry has not completely transformed itself, and while some countries have embraced reforms, corruption and avarice have become even more entrenched in others. Mining companies have often been the losers, and many have had to close down after suffering substantial losses. Human rights abuses of diamond diggers have been called out in a few countries. However, if one of the diamond industry's arch enemies, Global Witness, can admit grudgingly that improvements have been made, I take this as an impressive indicator of adaptation for the better.

A second reason for writing about these two industries is that there are interesting points of commonality or overlap between them. In recent years, the reformers in the diamond industry in Africa faced many problems of a similar nature to those of the aid industry, such as having to work with corrupt governments and powerful elites, and have engaged with each other on a number of matters in common. These include talks on development such as the Extractative Industries Transparency Initiative, which promotes open and accountable management of oil, gas, and mineral resources. Likewise all sides came together over the Kimberly Process Certification Scheme, which sought to halt the sale of blood diamonds.

The British aid agency at the time, the Overseas Development Administration, actually paid the fees of the chief diamond gamekeeper mentioned in this book. It may be that the direction of most criticism between the industries has been aid critiques of diamonds but not always. The diamond industry has occasionally been able to embarrass the aid industry, such as when it had clear evidence that one of the aid darlings, the leader of Rwanda, was responsible for ransacking diamonds in the Democratic Republic of the Congo.

As I mulled over the contrasts between these industries, I became convinced that it would be more interesting and illuminating to write about the changes over the years through personal stories – mine in the aid industry and Andy's (my husband) in diamonds. The conversations he and I have had – the questioning, challenges and critique we have put to each other –

weave through our working lives. Naturally we have learnt more about each other's line of work but we did not start from a zero baseline. My first encounter with the diamond industry dates from when I was five years old. Andy has encountered and talked with dozens of aid workers over the years, apparently telling them where they were going wrong which, he insists, they appreciated.

Andy used to enjoy provoking 'my people' because we are an easy target, mostly quite ignorant of what happens in the diamond industry in Africa, but prepared to be prejudiced nevertheless. His saying "I wiped the blood off the diamond I gave Ann" is sure to evoke a reaction - someone will always get on their high horse, wag a finger and harrumph about blood diamonds. He warned me "Don't wear the diamond ring in a hot shower or it will melt, "and then relented "Ok, you are carrying the GDP of a small African nation on your finger." Neither was true, but that was all part of his story-telling.

Characterwise, Andy and I are chalk and cheese. He is a raconteur to my analyst. He does not take life too seriously, whereas I tend to worry over details. In his self-denigrating fashion, he will claim his cv consists of one line: "My mother loves me." Mine runs to over ten pages and never mentions my mother. Andy has probably influenced my thinking more than I his, which I will admit I find a little aggravating. He has a great skill for cutting to the chase, slicing out the bullshit with which the aid industry is replete.

Attitudes are becoming far more polarised and entrenched in recent years, due to many factors including social media. Seeing the world in black and white is overriding shades of grey. There was a time when those in the aid industry could accept criticism of their work without the critic being regarded as supporting a conservative anti-aid camp, but I am not sure that this still holds true.

Institutional reputations tend to live on for far longer after practices and behaviour have changed. Aid continues to be seen generally as a force for good especially when NGOs are providing the aid, while the diamond industry is considered to be mired in graft and corruption. The 2006 film Blood Diamonds left its mark on the scandal over diamond association with conflict.

Plenty of academic writers, a few journalists, some practitioners, and senior aid officials have written books about aid – what it is, why it is given, what works and what doesn't. For about five years, I asked myself what I could add by writing a book. I have not run an aid agency; I rarely had access to senior officials; I am not an academic. But I have been one of the foot soldiers so to speak, either carrying out projects or evaluating how they were carried out, working in 17 countries in Africa and for many different organisations including several aid agencies and 19 companies. These projects all fall within what is often called long-term development aid rather than humanitarian assistance.

Having lived and studied in Italy, I became attuned to a way of thinking and rationalising the world where interests, incentives, and ways around rules are key to understanding behaviour, whereas I would say that many of my British colleagues over the years have held an idealistic, altruistic, and rules-bound view of what aid can do. For them, a moral imperative – we must help – trumps practical and pragmatic considerations, let alone the notion that perhaps aid produces the very opposite results to those anticipated.

Mine is a journey through my own realisation and self-awareness about the industry I worked in over a period of 30 years or so. I have tried to make sense of the contradictions and uncomfortable realities I faced and tell it through my own eyes as well as those of various colleagues and friends, European and African, who are aid workers and experts, journalists, academics or writers.

It was my idea to write a book, but as soon as I considered including the diamond angle I was keen to enlist my husband's participation. He was a little wary, and in the end I used his own arguments to encourage him to collaborate with me - "You claim you never say no to me" -shameless wheedling on my part.

Andy's story encompasses the sea change in the diamond industry. At a young age he worked in De Beers, buying diamonds from diamond traders and miners in a number of countries in Africa, often taking on huge responsibility and risk, which he has always downplayed. Instead, he chooses to focus on his grand adventures such as when, at the age of 24, he was shipping up to a million dollars of diamonds a week (around four million in today's prices), and fully capable of walking away from a lengthy negotiation – toting his waterskis and picnic hamper – as a tactic to conclude a deal. He knows the diamond business inside out, and at the height of his career in De Beers, he was Chief Executive for Sales in India.

Andy later worked for a man whom I have come to regard as a champion in the industry, providing advice and valuation services to African governments. Andy and his colleagues never touted their contributions to the positive changes in the diamond industry. They considered that the industry had to adapt, and they did not put any moral spin on those changes.

The story of diamonds is told through my conversations with Andy, his boss and another diamond valuer about their experiences and views. A google search of diamonds and conflict will come up with 1000s of hits but few of them are written by people with in depth knowledge of the industry as Andy and his colleagues have.

In writing this book, my aim has been to reach a wide audience. I wanted to make the aid issues and arguments come alive, and be of interest to people who know very little about the subject of aid by writing as much about the interesting, quirky, sometimes dangerous, and often absurd situations I and others found ourselves in as well as the sadly all too frequent duplication and waste of aid funds.

I also wanted to offer people a glimpse of what lies behind the shimmering world of sparkling diamond jewellery: excitement alongside desperate boredom, the risk of being betrayed and murdered, how the industry has supported greater African control over its resources for better or worse, and some of the truths and myths about blood diamonds.

I hope I have risen to the challenge of a former colleague, Mr P, who on hearing I was going to write a book about international aid said "just don't be boring." While there is inevitably some description and analysis of the two industries, I have left the detailed, more academic and practitioner accounts to the many other excellent writers on these subjects. The style is deliberately understated, flippant at times, because the aim is to inform and entertain while the sub-text is to challenge assumptions.

The chapters in the book alternate between stories of aid and of diamonds, at times bringing both together. Most but not all chapters focus on one country in Africa. Pithy and ironic conversations between Andy and me weave through the chapters, thereby linking the two industries. For each industry, the sequence of events charts a progression over time more or less. However, the story of diamonds starts at an earlier point in time to that of aid so there is some zig-zaging back and forth in time between these accounts of the two industries.

Chapter 1: A swamp in Sierra Leone

When I was five years old, my father started working for a diamond mining company in Sierra Leone. This was probably a rather unusual career change for him though it had geography in common with his earlier working life. He had been a war veteran of the Second World War, and stayed on in the British Army for a few years in Nigeria. This was followed by a job in Irlam Steel, near Manchester, but he was made redundant at a time when he was married and with three small children.

An old army friend of his told him that Sierra Leone Selection Trust was looking for ex-army officers to work in security, and he was quickly offered a job. Apparently their assumptions about former army officers were that they were a trustworthy lot and, like De Beers' search for the ideal buyer, they virtually cloned a security stereotype. The assumption generally proved correct, but there was quite a scandal when one of these supposedly trustworthy security officers stole some diamonds in Sierra Leone.

My first memories of Sierra Leone on getting out of the aircraft in Freetown are the heat, humidity, and buzzing sound of cicadas. My mother and we three girls carried on living in England because there were no suitable schools where my father was working upcountry in a place called Yengema, which meant swamp in the local language, but we would spend school holidays with our father there. Sierra Leone Selection Trust had built residential units right across its large operating perimeter and the centre of operations was the company's administrative offices and the Separator House, which were near to the one food store and a club house with swimming pool and tennis and squash courts. Beyond that, there were also golf and rugby clubs. Houses were standard-sized bungalows with air conditioning, and the whole area covered several square miles. The only transport for us was a rickety old bus, which would come by on a circuit every hour or so.

My sisters and I would spend all our time at the Yengema Club in the swimming pool while our mother read and sunbathed, lavishly applying Ambre Solaire factor 1 or 2, which probably had a similar effect to basting herself with cooking oil. It was certainly not intended to protect against the sun. Our bodies would quickly redden and burn, and we would take delight in peeling long stretches of skin off each other's backs. At Christmas, Santa Claus landed at the clubhouse in a helicopter, suffocating in his festive garb.

My first offer of marriage took place at this time: a group of Sierra Leonean boys barred the entrance to the girls' toilets and asked if I would marry one of them and take him back to England with me. This was the least romantic of the three marriage proposals I have had in my life though the second one, in the milk section of Tesco in Brixton, was hardly more auspicious.

Not surprisingly, my parents' marriage did not survive the lengthy separations, and from when I was about 12, my sisters and I would travel to Sierra Leone as unaccompanied children. Manoeuvring around the chaos at Freetown Airport was a struggle since the company did not send anyone to meet us there or to accompany us to a hotel and then onto road or air transport to Yengema. On one occasion, when I was about 15 years old and travelling with my younger sister (our older sister was 18, and no longer eligible for a free flight), I had to make a decision about whether or not to trust a stranger to give us a lift to our hotel in Freetown. We had starting talking to this man on the rusty old ferry between the airport and the city. He was an executive of Bata Shoes, and fortunately did as he had promised, though I remember a sickening moment when he stopped for some time at his house to drop off his luggage first, wondering if we had got ourselves into trouble.

When my mother was no longer around to look after us, we would spend all our time with other kids at the Yengema Club, swimming, chatting and hanging out, eating hamburgers and chips, and ordering rounds of Fanta and Coke, which I have happily never drunk since then. If our father was home alone briefly from his working shift over lunch, he would typically eat a huge plate of lettuce with maybe one radish, which came from his weekly rations from the company's vegetable gardens. This feast was crowned by a spoonful of salad cream. I remember that although he would always be very mournful before we left, a month or so later we would receive a stiff letter from him, appalled by the bill for all the food we had consumed during our stay, which we had signed for at the club.

At Christmas and Easter, there would be a party at the Rugby Club. While my father was knocking back drinks with his colleagues, I don't think it occurred to him that he should be keeping a watchful eye on what we girls were drinking. That sort of responsibility would have fallen under the purview of our mother. I know I used to drink several vodka and limes those evenings, and yet strangely I cannot remember ever feeling drunk.

While he was writing his book The Heart of the Matter about war, espionage, adultery, and betrayal in Sierra Leone, Graham Greene travelled to Yengema, and his description of the heat and humidity, the class snobbery and permanent state of drunkenness among the Europeans was spot on. My father worked in Sierra Leone for 13 years until his retirement, and I have had plenty of time since then to reflect on how unrewarding and restricted his life must have been. Although I may doubt that he was up to the task of looking after teenage girls nearly 50 years younger than he was, I am convinced that he felt he was doing his duty as the breadwinning father by working in this thankless and monotonous job stoically and uncomplainingly in order to support us.

When I was 15 or 16, I had a crush on my father's young boss, who offered to show me and my younger sister some diamonds. Because I asked so many questions –

trying to prolong precious time spent in his company - he suggested we join his men when they went up on a helicopter to deter illicit diamond miners. The helicopter flew low and swooped down on Sierra Leoneans as they sifted through fine particles on the river banks looking for alluvial diamonds. The men and women ran helter-skelter at our approach, and now I look back on that trip with a sense of discomfort, which I think I was vaguely aware of at the time. The company had purchased a licence from the government to mine diamonds, but given they were mainly alluvial (meaning they were found along rivers rather than deep down underground), it could not fence off a vast area. Was it really necessary to bear down so aggressively on these local people who would hardly have been able to gather many precious stones?

On one occasion, my father accused a Sierra Leonean of stealing a diamond in the Separator House, which was where diamonds were separated from the gravel. This man turned around and accused my father. The upshot was that my father was locked up in the local prison for a few months. A judge came up from Freetown once a month and let my father out after there was no case officially put against him. I don't recall my father ever talking about conditions in that prison, but then I don't remember him ever describing his life as a prisoner of war in Germany's Sudetenland either. I used to rail against his old-fashioned, fuddy-duddy views when I was young, but I am glad to have had time to know and respect him in later years before his demise at the ripe old age of 93.

As a young adult, I was often an outsider, a lonely place to be as a youngster though it can also foster an enquiring mind, more likely to question what the majority considers good, bad, right or wrong. We were outsiders at our local grammar school, the only children who spent the holidays in West Africa or indeed anywhere abroad. After school I studied politics at Exeter University, where I campaigned to improve the conditions of students, women especially. But I was also a research assistant to a professor of international politics, who was a former major-general and expert in counter-insurgency.

An inspiring American female professor told me about the university founded by the member states of the European Community, the European University Institute. To be considered for a postgraduate grant there, one needed an interesting research topic and at least a second European language. However, it turned out that a mosquito bite on the eye the night before the interview also helps. Apparently I was one of just two prospective candidates who had applied with a women's studies topic. I was told later that while the other candidate had been considered a bit abrasive (more likely assertive), I had been seen as sympathetic. Actually, I had decided to court the sympathy of the all-male interview panel by explaining the reason for having one closed eye and, as I hoped, they were instantly charming.

So once again I found myself rather alone, this time in my non-mainstream research on the sociology of childlessness. A famous British professor of sociology once told me that this was a non-subject, because of course all women want to have children. However, thirty five years after I completed my PhD, the childfree lifestyle has become quite common.

I started going out with an Italian, Maurizio. I think I fell for his wonderful large family, grandpa included, as much as him. When he landed a job with the United Nations High Commissioner of Refugees and was posted to Mozambique, he suggested I accompany him. We spent two years there during the civil war, which was not an easy time for the country nor for us to adapt to a very different way of living so far from family and friends. Our argumentative characters came to the fore, but we got through those years somehow or other. His second posting was in Guinea. We got married, went to Guinea in 1994 and that is where my story begins.

Chapter 2: Guinea - Baptism by fire and the World Bank Debt Tables

Andy's and my paths first crossed for a fleeting moment in Guinea. I was going out for the evening and he had been invited to my host's home for dinner. He enjoys rebuking me for the fact that I don't recall meeting him then, whereas he remembered me.

Located on the west coast of Africa, Guinea is a predominantly tropical country with a monsoonal-type rainy season lasting half the year, warm temperatures, and high humidity. Conakry, the capital, lies on the coast, looking like a 36-kilometre-long arm finishing in a fist jutting out from the mainland, sandwiched between mangrove swamps.

In July and August alone there are about two metres of rain, half the annual rainfall. Imagine trying to move anywhere, even down the road, when it is raining so hard and the roads are inundated. It is hellish. Everything is perpetually damp. It is difficult to dry clothing, and anything left in a cupboard or a wardrobe for a week or so quickly develops a grey-blue mould. If you sit in a chair without moving, sweat starts to trickle down your arms. Guinea was one of those African countries which everyone in the know in the aid industry avoided like the plague.

Historically, Guinea was on the edges of the major West African empires, especially Ghana and Mali. France had replaced Portugal as the dominant European power in the region, and in the notorious European carve-up of Africa in the last part of the 19th century, France negotiated Guinea's present boundaries. It gained independence in 1958.

Two strongmen dominated Guinea after independence, and both left a legacy of extreme personalisation of power and violent suppression of opponents. Guinea's leader at independence was Sékou Touré, a radical and authoritarian Pan-Africanist, hailed by some as a hero, by others as a tyrant. He ruled for 25 years. After his death, a military coup resulted in Guinea's second strongman, Lansana Conté, who ruled for 24 years till he died in 2008.[1]

Guinea attained notoriety as the only country among France's former French colonies in Africa – the Federation of French West Africa – which refused to accept de Gaulle's referendum proposal that these colonies accept "local autonomy within the newly created French Community." The Guinean 'non' vote resulted in total and immediate independence, and became the basis of the heroic myth and revolutionary image of Sékou Touré."[2]

The Washington Post wrote about France brutally tearing down all that they considered their contributions to

Guinea: "In reaction, and as a warning to other French-speaking territories, the French pulled out of Guinea over a two-month period, taking everything they could with them. They unscrewed light bulbs, removed plans for sewage pipelines in Conakry, and even burned medicines rather than leave them for the Guineans."[3]

After Independence, President Ahmed Sékou Touré adopted a socialist model. He established close ties with the Soviet Union, but during the 1960s he moved away from the USSR before conducting a collectivist experiment inspired by Maoist China. This proved to be a failure, and in 1984 it was estimated that two million Guineans, of whom about half were refugees from Sierra Leone or Liberia, had gone into exile in neighbouring countries or further afield.[4]

The Boiro Camp or Camp Mamadou-Boiro (1960 – 1984) was a gendarmerie camp created at the time of French colonisation, which became a military internment, torture, and death camp for Guinea under the regime of Sékou Touré. It was known as the Auschwitz of the Guineans, and Amnesty International estimates that 50,000 people died there, decimating the Guinean elite.[5]

In November 1970, Portuguese troops assisted by Guinean dissidents attempted to overthrow the Sékou Touré regime to neutralise the rebels active in Guinea-Bissau, and to free Portuguese prisoners held in Conakry. The operation had mixed success, and in 1971 Touré subjected the country to severe repression. People opposed to the regime were accused of subversion, arrested, and stood secret trials, in some cases followed by summary executions.[6] On January 25, 1971, about 100 Guineans were executed in the early morning in Conakry at the so-called 'pont dit des pendus' (bridge of the hanged men).

A friend of mine, Maurice, an urbane diplomat and banker and now a neighbour, was among the few foreigners to visit Guinea in the 1970s. It was impossible to acquire a visa through the formal channels, and he was eventually assisted by the London Diamond Corporation, but his arrival by plane from Senegal was ominous: he saw several tails of smashed planes in the swamps around Conakry airport. Maurice was the first person to stay in the hotel built to host the Organisation of African Unity, the Independence, which was next door to Camp Mamadou-Bouro, and from the ground floor of the hotel he could hear the prisoners' screams.

One evening Maurice was ordered to attend a performance of the African Ballet Company. The person sitting next to him turned out to be the Minister of Defence, responsible for the camp, and the main guests were North Vietnamese. Maurice got talking with a wizened old man who announced at the end "Thank God, I couldn't stand much more of this." A photograph of them both appeared the following day in the Hanoi newspapers, and Maurice said rather ruefully that the old man turned out to be the infamous General Giap of the People's Army of North Vietnam and he got hell from the Foreign Office.[7]

When he was working in the World Bank in the 1980s, Maurice returned to Guinea to unravel a contract that the Guinean government had made with the Soviet Union. The latter had insisted that it be based on barter rather than monetary payment, so the Soviet Union rather conveniently acquired bauxite while Guinea less conveniently got snow ploughs and tinned sardines in exchange.

In 1975, Touré prohibited all private trade in a decree stating that agricultural products must be delivered by state cooperatives. At this point, the market women shouted 'Non!' Their famous August 1977 revolt in Conakry market proved to be Touré's downfall, and a turning point for the regime in terms of the role played by the state in the economy. The women formed committees to mobilise the population to campaign against the high cost of food and economic instability, and the revolt spread to the rest of the country. Riots broke out and some provincial governors were killed. Later that year, Touré legalised small businesses, and in 1978 diplomatic ties were re-established with France.

I can see these women in my mind's eye because I have known their sisters in other markets. They are dressed in layers of fabric, flamboyant and boldly coloured, clashing with flair. A baby is attached to their back with a wrap around their body in yet another bold and striking fabric.

They are large and buxom, and when they stand their ground they are formidable, like a tank, and they won't put up with shit from anyone. They will say to soldiers or anyone else in authority "I know your mamma. You go home and leave us in peace."

One of the legacies of the mass arrests and covert trials was that we foreigners found Guinean society to be very secretive and closed. The ghosts of the past pervaded the present, and as soon as I arrived, I felt the oppressive atmosphere. There was a tendency to never look anyone in the eye, there was no light-hearted banter, and people were very guarded in what they said and did.

Telephones were tapped, and it was well known that a local staff member in each foreign agency spied on foreigners. Val Treitlein, the Honorary British Counsel and one of just a handful of British nationals living in Guinea, once told a story about the phone tapping: she had called another woman to cancel a game of tennis. When her friend did not reply, Val spoke down the phone into the void "Could you tell my friend I cannot play tennis with her today?" There was no reply, but the friend was contacted by the spies who passed on her message.

The widespread practice of magic added to the strange quality of relationships in Guinea. My Italian husband Maurizio made friends with a couple of young Guinean men, and after a while these friends started to tell us about *marabouts* in Guinea. A marabout is a Muslim religious leader and teacher who historically had the function of a chaplain serving as a part of an Islamic army, but in Sub-Saharan Africa the marabout can carry a more negative connotation: a sorcerer, a bewitcher, or a soothsayer. If you want to hurt someone, you can pay a marabout to harm them in some more or less obvious way. For instance, a healthy young person may suddenly become poorly or die unexpectedly from an unknown illness.

Equally, if you suspect that someone is trying to harm you, you can obtain a safety charm called a *gri-gri* from a marabout to protect yourself, but in order for the spells to work, one has to believe, or at least be open to the possibility that marabout works. It was said that foreigners who flew in and out of the country could not fall under the influence of marabout, but those who lived there who received a constant drip-drip of inexplicable happenings and strange stories would start to fear that harm could come to them. The slightest suggestion could be enough to make them fall victim. I suppose it is not very different from the beliefs we hold in the developed world when it comes to medicine. The psychosomatic effect can be very powerful.

One story that intrigued me was about an elderly man who went to a cinema in a town called Labé. A young couple were talking to each other during the film, so the man leant forward and asked them politely to be quiet. They ignored him, and he asked them again to no avail. The next morning, the girl woke in her parents' home to find that she had male genitalia, and the boy in his parents' home discovered he had female genitalia. After the initial shock, both sets of parents started asking the kids questions: where had they been, what had they done, had they upset anyone? After a while, someone recalled that a well-known marabout who visited the town once a week had been at the cinema the evening before. Both sets of parents waited until the following week and went to pay a call on the marabout. They beseeched him to undo his spell, and they brought their kids to apologise for their behaviour. Respect duly paid, the marabout deigned to swap back the genitalia.

In addition to different beliefs and influences, I experienced acute aesthetic deprivation. It is only in recent years that neuroscience has started to take an interest in the importance of beauty, and one neuroscientist, Anjan Chatterjee, has researched the importance of beauty in people, landscapes and architecture.[8] Apparently, beauty detectors ping every time we see something we consider beautiful, and beauty is closely related to what we find good. My beauty sensors were taking a long break during this period. I do not say this as a privileged European who has never visited an impoverished part of the world, because that certainly was not true even then. There is naturally some element of subjectivity in everyone's perception of beauty, and I would acknowledge that most Guineans in Conakry did not feel the same sense of aesthetic deprivation that I experienced in their city, but the other overwhelming feeling I had in Conakry was that there was nothing of any beauty.

The intense rainfall resulted in paintwork eroding quickly on buildings, making most of the capital look as if it were in need of several layers of paint. There were no attractive buildings, old or new, as far as I could see. There were no parks. With one exception – a French café called Le Damier, which seemed to have been plucked out of a smart French city and dumped in error into Conakry, that served exquisite French pastries and handmade chocolates - there were no cafés, restaurants or cultural establishments. Opposite le Damier was the central market, where Andy used to buy Cuban cigars for a fraction of the usual price. After a gap of several years he returned to Conakry, and as he was being driven past the market in a taxi the same young boys spotted him in an instant, flagged him down and asked if he wanted Montecristos! They were quite willing to hand him boxes of them there and then, trusting that they would meet up with him later in his hotel to negotiate the price.

Vast rubbish dumps by the side of roads were pawed over by packs of stray rabid dogs. The sand on the beaches had been removed for road-building purposes, so all that was left were rocks and mud, and as a result no one spent any time at the beach.

We lived initially in a gated compound for UN agency staff - large flats with the bare minimum of furniture, a swimming pool, and a small lawn, and compared to the rest of the city this seemed quite attractive. I remember spending time in the early weeks by the pool, plucking delicate petals from the intoxicating frangipani trees, twirling them around in my fingers and inhaling the scent. Ping went my beauty sensor, but it did not last long.

Within a month of arriving in this rather depressing town, I was delighted to have a job to escape to. Knowing that I initially hated living in Mozambique without any work, Maurizio had looked for a job for me before I arrived. A Frenchwoman about to leave the World Bank was looking for a replacement. An introduction was made and I got the job. This sounds grander than it was, because while the majority of career postings in the World Bank are acquired through tough international competition, some locally hired personnel could acquire a short-term contract simply by being in a country at the right time and having a certain level of qualifications.

Before long, I was out of the frying pan and into the fire: from my arrival at the World Bank's offices - the Resident Mission - I had a lot to do and very little knowledge of how to do it. I had three colleagues, each of whom was totally different from the others and who didn't really like each other. The boss, Eduardo, was half Italian, half Uruguayan, rather typical of many staff in international bodies, which are replete with people toting several nationalities and languages. At a later time, I reflected that these varied national backgrounds with multilingual skill sets appeared to be the only requirement for such jobs.

Eduardo was reasonably friendly, but expected me to get up and running quickly. I later discovered when I travelled upcountry that he assigned to me the most uncomfortable Toyota pickup truck that he had purchased cheaply and unwisely for the resident mission. Somebody had to make use of this vehicle, so apparently my back could be sacrificed in the absence of any suspension. Furthermore, I would be allotted the driver who never washed and drove at breakneck speed, narrowly avoiding killing people in towns and villages. Since Eduardo was the kind of man who would open doors for a woman and rush to offer her a seat, this two-faced behaviour irked but did not surprise me.

Joseph, the Agricultural Officer, was an Israeli. He travelled frequently, and was quite knowledgeable about the country, but intolerant of anyone who spent most of their time in the office. At that time, the World Bank was largely centralised in its headquarters in Washington, DC, and it was said that the main function of the resident missions was as a 'boîte postale' or post box to ferry communications and documents between the team leaders and managers in Washington and their government counterparts here. Joseph clearly saw himself as playing a more active role, and advised me to do so too.

One piece of useful advice was to ensure that I was comfortable when travelling, otherwise I would find reasons not to leave the office. The comfort tips ranged from taking food and drink with me and a portable mosquito net to wearing long skirts so that I could squat in the bush without feeling awkward. The latter was especially pertinent because no matter how deserted the countryside appeared to be while being driven, the minute I gave in to the bursting need to pee the countryside bustled with all manner of local folk.

Less useful was his advice to read the World Bank Debt Tables to get a better idea of what the Bank did. These weighty tomes contained hundreds if not thousands of pages of numbers, and were complete gibberish to me, although they inspired me when I was trying to put pressure on my boss to push for a relocation allowance, the $5,000 sum usually allocated to internationally appointed staff in the resident missions. My right to this allowance lay in a grey area.

One day, I drew a simple cartoon of myself sitting in an empty flat with nothing except some large books piled on a table in front of me. The bubble caption coming out of my head read 'Ann was so bored in her empty flat that she even started reading the World Bank Debt Tables. When would her relocation allowance arrive?' I took a gamble and handed it to my boss. As I walked out of his office, he started chuckling and when I got back to mine I saw a one-line email he had dashed off to a colleague in Washington. The relocation allowance was granted,

29

though by then it was more essential to use it to purchase a car, which I would not have needed with an international appointment.

The other staff member was Cherif, a Guinean, one of whose portfolios had been handed to me, the social sector (predominantly health and education programmes), while he was re-assigned to the economic sector. I got on best of all with Cherif, with whom I felt safe to admit my total ignorance and plead for help. Cherif was non-judgmental, pragmatic, and happy to give advice on a daily basis. He would tell me the main things to do to avoid censure, which included always responding to emails from Washington the same day.

It was Ramadan, the Muslim fasting period, shortly after I started my job. I felt a little guilty about eating when most people around me were fasting. Someone pointed me in the direction of a café near our office at the end of a residential road. Opening the door, I had the urge to smile. Dozens of pairs of eyes darted anxiously up at me only to drop in relief at seeing a white foreigner enter the restaurant who was clearly not intent on reporting their religious shortcomings. I was reminded of a scene from Luis Bunuel's film The Phantom of Liberty in which bourgeois guests arrive at a dinner with a difference: everyone sits at a toilet placed around the dining room table and continues their conversation at ease with each other. At a certain point, one guest excuses himself and goes down the hallway to a small room. He locks himself inside, sits down at a small table and starts scoffing down a meal, looking slightly alarmed when another guest comes to try the door. When Cherif spotted a packet of biscuits in my office one day. I was apologetic, but he said "So what?" as he helped himself and stuffed down a couple of biscuits, which earned him a wry smile.

At other times, a woman provided meals cooked on a makeshift charcoal stove in the carpark of the World Bank. It was usually fried fish and jollof rice, made with the local short grain white rice, onions, tomatoes and probably some spice, and was delicious despite the less than desirable setting. I have never been able to make such good jollof rice since then, but perhaps that is because my attempts lack the added ingredient of diesel fumes.

To carry out my 'boite postale' tasks, from day one I began to receive messages from the Task Leaders in Washington. There was no introduction, no conversation, and while some of them visited the country months later, I never met others. Emails were brusque: "Ann - pass on these contractual documents and request the Minister's signature." "Pick up a procurement dossier from another ministry," etc. Without hearing someone's voice or having any idea of what sort of person they were, it was difficult to know how to relate to them. I was unsure whether I should at times admit that I didn't understand what they expected from me. Could I exchange pleasantries with them about the weather in Washington for instance? Should I ask them how they were, wish them a happy Christmas, etc.? It seemed safer to drop by Cherif's office for advice.

I was invited to a number of meetings of the United Nations Development Programme, the UN's development arm which went under the acronym UNDP. On occasion, they ran week-long workshops on subjects like poverty reduction. I didn't see how I could usefully contribute or take any findings back to our Task Leaders in Washington, and was tempted not to go. Cherif advised me "Those workshops are a waste of time. The UNDP has no funding to do anything substantial, but it keeps member states happy by hiring local consultants to write papers and facilitate workshops. Public servants are glad of the chance to be out of their offices and eat a good lunch. But you must put in an appearance at the start, middle, and end of the week. If you don't, the UN will complain to the World Bank that we are not coordinating our programmes, and this will come back to bite you."

The main task I had been assigned was a relatively new job in the Bank: Non Governmental Organisation (NGO) Liaison Officer. About that time, the Bank had been heavily criticised by NGOs for exacerbating poverty. A campaigning group of NGOs called 50 Years is Enough claimed that the Bank's structural adjustment programmes[9] in poor countries were making life even harder for the poor rather than improving economies. The highly vaunted trickle-down effect to the poor wasn't happening. The newly appointed Bank President

James Wolfensohn committed the Bank to responding to these criticisms, and one of his initiatives was to appoint NGO Liaison Officers in the Resident Missions. Their job was to contact and meet NGOs in the country and report back to Washington every month at the highest level, to Vice-President Jean-Louis Sarbib.

This was rather a daunting task, and I had no idea how I should go about it. Again, Cherif was helpful in giving me names of a few of the better-known NGOs, while at the same time offering his opinion of them. Most of them were just in it for the money, he said, and didn't represent any 'constituency' of poor people. In any case, the Bank was not set up to give funding to these bodies; it gave grants and credits to governments. The government agencies could choose to contract NGOs to take part in their programmes, but that was up to them.

Many of the NGO personnel were, he told me, former public servants who had lost their jobs when the Bank's structural adjustment programmes contracted the size of the public service. They were not people who lived among or were committed to helping and empowering the poor. But if the latest development fashion among the Bank and other international agencies was to 'be nice' and give funding to NGOs, former public servants might as well adapt and set up a NGO.

At this time in Washington, the eager beavers who were already fully signed up to working with NGOs came up with policy notes, tools, and training on how to engage with poor people through NGOs. The buzz words were 'participation' and 'participatory rural appraisal', which were all about differentiating between mere consultation with poorer people (not good – their views could and would be ignored) to joint decision-making between those people and decision-makers, such as local or central government (good – this would supposedly empower them).

The Bank produced a book called 'Participation and Social Assessment: Tools and Techniques' in 1996, which ran to 347 pages. Glancing through it, I thought this is far too long, the tools and techniques proposed are far too time-consuming, no one is going to read it, and they are going to make things up as they go along. Some of the interview questions proposed had me cringing even then, and I can imagine that had I known Andy at the time, he would have taken delight in parodying me by asking those very questions in his poshest elderly lady accent, adding a few extra comments to thereby render them completely ridiculous: "Hello you poor people, it is rather hot here isn't it? Could I just ask you to be so kind as to describe a poor family? And the life of a poor person? And would you by any chance know any good stories or proverbs about poverty? I'm sure you must do."

I soon discovered from perusing a few of the other NGO Liaison Officer reports that most of them were simply inviting a lot of NGOs to the resident mission or a larger meeting venue to meet them, hear about their projects and tell them what the Bank was doing. The thrust of this minimalistic approach was numbers: give tea and biscuits to as many complaining NGOs as possible, and then send them on their way. Despite being harsh critics of the Bank from afar, once invited in they tended to assume a polite demeanour. In any case it was usually the big international NGOs that were most disparaging, and we had very few of those in Guinea.

After holding a few of these meetings, the enquiring sociologist in me felt that I hadn't grasped anything of real value to tell the Team Leaders in Washington. I once caved into the Bank's gender agenda by inviting so-called women's NGOs to a meeting, but upon discovering that most of them were wives of politicians or diplomats, it was clear that they were definitely not champions of poor women.

I also met some of the NGO leaders individually in the Bank's office. They were usually men, elderly at that, often wearing their 'grand boubou', a flowing robe which can signify a certain elevated status such as a person who has made the Haj pilgrimage to Mecca. I learnt a few phrases in one Guinean language, Perl, and was advised that it was a good idea to spend the first few minutes repeating these greetings rather than being so indelicate as to launch straight into the purpose of the meeting.

The routine went "Hello, how are you? How is your family? Did you sleep well (though it surprised me that this question could be considered a suitable one)? And how are you?" I felt rather than knew that being a young woman talking with an older Guinean man involved rather tricky sexual power dynamics. Introducing myself as Doctor Condy (although the Bank only uses the title for medical staff since most people have PhDs) seemed a wise move.

With support and contacts from Cherif and Joseph, I began to go on week-long visits to NGOs outside the capital, to see what they were doing, ask questions, and meet the people they were helping. It was difficult to know if this more qualitative approach was appreciated or not back at HQ, but it seemed to me essential if what I did was to make any sense outside of box ticking.

It is often only in retrospect that one feels one has learnt something useful in life. At the time, I experienced so many layers of incomprehension and I tried my hardest to be polite, enquiring, and not let slip how little I knew. This was mentally exhausting. Not knowing the job or the organisation I was working for was one layer, not speaking any more than a few words of the various Guinean languages was another (upcountry, few people spoke French, and even then my French and their French were dissimilar), and not understanding a culture steeped in the murky shadows of the former Sékou Touré regime was yet another.

When you ask a villager or farmer a question even in your own culture, there are many assumptions at play. The villagers may assume that your real interest lies elsewhere, but you are obliged to or feel it is more tactful to ask this question. They guess how much or little you want to know, but may expect that since you are from a different and wealthier, more privileged background you won't understand their situation anyhow and the question/answer exchange is simply an opportunity to repeat mantras that may be acceptable.

For instance, the typical answer to a question about why children were not in school was "we are poor", which was certainly part of the explanation, but when I was able to dig a little deeper the range of issues included, in addition to the obvious opportunity-cost issue – meaning that if kids are in school, they are not helping in the fields – the lack of latrines posing problems for menstruating girls; male teachers seducing girls, girls being attacked on the way to school, the teachers being incompetent and apparently not teaching the children anything of any value.

As I later realised, village chiefs are usually told when foreigners will be in town and given the foreigners' latest aid agenda (e.g. gender, HIV/AIDS, etc.). They would instruct the villagers to use these key words even if they didn't understand what they meant or felt something else such as a failed harvest or crop predators were the most pressing matters in their lives. My questions would be translated by the NGO representative, often using remarkably few words compared to mine. I soon realised that I hadn't a hope in hell of communicating in any meaningful way.

The other challenge I had to deal with was my husband Maurizio's strange behaviour. After I had been working for barely a month, he arrived home to announce out of the blue that he had resigned from his job in the United Nations High Commission for Refugees. No amount of prodding from me would make him admit why he had resigned, why he had done so without telling me, and what he proposed we do next. He just kept insisting that he hated being in Guinea and wanted us to go back to the UK. This seemed to me out of the question because we had burnt our bridges. I had given up my job, put our belongings into storage, and rented out our flat. He had no job to go to and I might well struggle to find a new job.

In a situation like ours in Guinea, his job was an 'international' posting with good pay and benefits, such as the right to live in UN accommodation. Mine was a consultancy with a low monthly salary and no benefits. For a couple of months we rented a room in a house with someone he had worked with, a woman who seemed remarkably unfriendly to us, and especially to him.

I think I felt that trying to get to the bottom of this conundrum with Maurizio on top of my demanding job was too difficult. Maybe I was lazy, and I certainly didn't want to argue with him given his propensity to lash out verbally. It went through my mind that he was having an affair with another woman, but I dismissed this possibility given he seemed so eager to leave the country. So he mooched about the house while I went out to work. Then he managed to find an offer of a short-term contract in Angola and was very keen to take it. There was no question of me accompanying him, so I suggested that he went and I stayed.

Social psychology has in recent years recognised that not all delusions are harmful; on the contrary, individuals and nation states need 'useful delusions' because they serve an important psychological function in keeping us sane[10]. My useful delusion was that my marriage was fundamentally fine, but just going through a rocky period.

Before leaving, and realising that I was not very happy in my lodgings, Maurizio sought an arrangement for me to move into the house of a Dutchman he knew, who was the local KLM director and Honorary Dutch Consul.

After my shoddy, mosquito-ridden accommodation, Robert's house was palatial. Everything was in pristine condition. I remember walking in with my few belongings, and feeling awkwardly that I was making the place dirty by my very presence - my dusty shoes and suitcases, and sweaty, creased and clinging clothes.

Here there were white rugs, immaculate sofas, shiny tiled floors, beautiful furniture, ornaments and paintings, a state of the art kitchen, and – bliss for me – air conditioning that was kept at a constant 21-22 degrees. Four or five full-time staff tended to Robert's every need and whim. The house was scrubbed within inches of its life, cushions were puffed up several times a day, floors were polished till they shone like a mirror and you could have eaten a meal off them. A driver would chauffeur him around in a car, which was thoroughly cleaned at the start of each day, inside and out. Meals were delicious, prepared with ingredients that had been flown in on KLM flights, not just what had been found that day in the local market.

Robert always dressed impeccably as if he were about to attend a reception: a suit, starched shirt, tie, and polished shoes. Even at the weekends he wore very smart casual clothes. As a diplomat, he would be invited to various social events, and I accompanied him to some of them. Protocol dictated that he must sit on the Dutch flag side of the car on the back seat, while I sat next to him.

Shortly after Maurizio had left, I received an urgent request at work. An NGO had contacted President Wolfensohn directly to ask how the Bank could support it. This was a very smart move, possibly the first time an African NGO had ever written to the Bank's President. Its effect was immediate. The Bank hit DEFCON 1 button, staff were galvanised, and I was ordered to find the organisation immediately.

I spent my Christmas Day that year racing around Conakry trying to track down the NGO. The address was of little use given few streets are named, and even when they are their whereabouts is unknown to all but a few. After trying a number of sources to no avail, I hit on the obvious solution: given the NGO writer stated that they were refugees, I went to United Nations High Commissioner for Refugees. There I was given directions.

When I finally turned up at the house of this organisation, I was inwardly spitting bullets while outwardly plastering a brilliant smile on my face and applying my silkiest voice. It turned out that this NGO was just one extended family of Sierra Leonians who hoped to find some kind of gainful employment while they were in Guinea. They did not represent any kind of 'civil society working to support local development' and, whilst I could feel sorry for them, I was pretty certain that the World Bank would have no interest in and no mandate to do anything for them. I rushed back to my office to dispatch an email of my findings to Washington, and could then finally settle down to a festive drink.

Robert and I would take a boat across to a nearby island sometimes at weekends, the Iles de Los, one of which had the reputation of being the original Treasure Island. In 1904, the British owned these islands, before handing them over to France in exchange for Britain relinquishing fishing rights in Newfoundland and Labrador. While Robert Louis Stephenson was writing his book Treasure Island, he spent some time on the island of Roume, and it is believed that the story was based on a British pirate by the name of Crawford, who was captured by the British navy and hanged in Conakry.[11]

There was a pretty beach with clean sand, a restaurant and hotel with residential beach huts, where I met a couple of diamond buyers. One of them, Bob Gollifer, was funny, a breath of fresh air, and a reminder of the joys of self-deprecating British humour. He would be in the sea calling out to me to get into the water just at the very moment when he knew that I would be hit by an enormous wave and tossed back up the beach. "Come on, you can make it, Ann," he would say with patent insincerity, barely suppressing a giggle. The oppression of Conakry appeared to lift while I was there. I told Bob about my father's experience in Sierra Leone. He was surprised that I knew something about the diamond industry. I learnt later that the circles of those working in development aid rarely overlapped with the diamond industry. In the eyes of many aid workers, diamond mining appeared to be on a par with the evils of weapons manufacturing or tobacco.

Bob too had his story about the particularities of working in Guinea. De Beers had sent one of their most successful buyers from the Congo to Guinea, and it had been a disaster:

"The buyers in the Congo really spoke down to the clients and they could get away with it. But in Guinea, the Guineans had kicked out the French and they expected a modicum of respect from the white man and rightfully so. Will didn't realise this and applied his usual behaviour from working in the Congo, so the clients stopped turning up and started selling more cheaply to the Armenians. Each time they sold a shipment, they would drop into his office to let him know that they had sold more cheaply to his competitors because they, the Armenians, had shown them courtesy.

"Will started drinking a bottle of whisky a day and abusing his flatmate. One of my mates heard about it and had him psycho-evac'd out[12], but as soon as Will got off the plane in Heathrow the cold air sobered him up, and he appeared to be fine again. De Beers thought there was nothing wrong with him and sent him straight back to Guinea, but a day later he had gone mad again, and had to be re-psycho-evac'd out.

"It's an important story about respecting people - and they knew more about the price of diamonds than we did. In the Congo they didn't know the prices - they were idiots - but everywhere else in West Africa they normally did. They had been doing it for the last 50 to 60 years. It's one of those things about life. Will took himself too seriously and it was all about his own ego, he was a self-important prick."

In the months to come, life seemed a little easier, even while I was aware that my relationship with Maurizio was at a strange impasse. I became friends with Val Treitlein, the Honorary British Consul, and her family, and enjoyed their entertaining a wide array of acquaintances who ranged from elusive coffee dealers to Russian diplomats. The latter would arrive bearing extravagant gifts of vodka and caviar. Val had only been able to enjoy a discreet friendship with the Russians during the Soviet era, and the fall of the Iron Curtain made it easier to see them.

I went to a Russian artist for lessons in watercolour painting. Fortunately, the limited communication between us did not prove an obstacle, and with her support I developed a lifelong interest in painting.

The Bank's Education Team Leader came to Guinea, so I finally had a chance to meet one of my bosses. Philip was one of those committed individuals who clearly believed in what the Bank could do to improve peoples' lives, and refused to allow money to be wasted on him. He declined the Bank's business travel allowance and flew economy. He had identified a significant commitment to girls' education in the Minister of Education, Aicha Bah Diallo, and did what he could to use and if necessary bend Bank rules to help her achieve her goals.

Because of Guinea's poor relationship with France, there were very few foreign donors and aid programmes in Guinea, which I realised later made this country quite unique. And it was also clear that in education the Bank's support made a difference. Over just an eight-year period (1989 to 1996), Guinea managed to double the number of girls enrolled in schools, from 113,000 to 233,000.[13] Again, it was only later that I appreciated I had had the good fortune to see all the right ingredients in place for such a highly successful project.

Before the end of my year-long contract with the Bank, Robert left Conakry and I had to leave his comfortable house. I moved into a small one-bedroom apartment above a Chinese restaurant by the infamous bridge of the hanged men. Not a good omen. I was back with my few belongings in a sparsely furnished flat.

I went on my furthest trip to a place called Siguiri in the gold mining area of Guinea, near the border with Mali. The journey lasted from dawn to dusk, with the last four hours spent covering just 40 miles due to flooded roads with deep potholes. Fortunately, I was travelling in a car owned by the NGO accompanying me with rather better suspension than the Bank's Toyota. Some of this journey was through magnificent countryside with escarpments, rivers (Siguiri itself is on the banks of the River Niger), magnificent trees such as the ficus magnolia with its extensive tentacles and mango trees giving shade to groups of local farmers.

I cannot recall now the purpose of that trip, but I remember only too well arriving back at my flat. After the exhaustion and stiffness from the 15-hour road trip, I stumbled up the stairs and when I opened the door the first things I saw were my wedding photos on the coffee table, spread out in a neat circle. I felt alarm and a clammy sense of shock because I knew I did not have those photographs with me in Guinea - and yet there they were. My first instinct was to call out Maurizio's name - but of course he was not there. The circular arrangement of the photographs seemed symbolic - as if my marriage was being returned to me, no longer wanted.

I asked my cleaner if he had put the photos on the table, and he denied it but he would not look me in the eye. Then I met up with a Belgian woman, Sophie, who worked in the Ministry of Women's Affairs, which was a high temple of gossip about marabout magic. She told me my husband was having an affair with his Guinean secretary, a woman who was known to practise marabout. Sophie had been unsure whether to tell me or not, but after hearing that this woman had just returned from spending a week with Maurizio in Angola, she felt the relationship was serious enough for me to know about.

The shock of this news was compounded by the realisation that since I knew Maurizio had those wedding photographs, she had evidently brought them back to Guinea. According to Sophie, marabouts deliver their messages via an elderly man, and the guards in my building confirmed that an unknown old man had come to my flat while my cleaner was there and I was away.

There are many ways in which dysfunctional relationships come to an end (or maybe worse still, do not end but persist unhappily), but this was probably among the scariest of ruptures. Shortly after, my contract came to an end and I was delighted to leave Guinea. It is one country I have never had any desire to return to, despite learning so much during that year.

Chapter 3: Diamonds in the Wild West of Zaire

"The Zairois thought there was no number above 100,000 - after that we negotiated heatedly over baseball caps and T-shirts."

Diamonds have a long history as beautiful objects of desire. In the first century AD, the Roman naturalist Pliny stated: "Diamond is the most valuable, not only of precious stones, but of all things in this world."

The world's love of diamonds started in India, where diamonds were gathered from the country's rivers and streams. India was trading in diamonds possibly as early as the fourth century BC. The country's resources yielded limited quantities for an equally limited market – India's very wealthy. Gradually this changed. Indian diamonds found their way, along with other exotic merchandise, to Western Europe in the caravans that traveled to Venice's medieval markets. By the 1400s, diamonds were becoming fashionable accessories for Europe's elite. In the early 1700s, as India's diamond supplies began to decline, Brazil emerged as an important source.

The story of the modern diamond market really begins on the African continent, with the 1866 discovery of diamonds in Kimberley, South Africa. The entrepreneur Cecil Rhodes established De Beers Consolidated Mines Limited in 1888. By 1900, De Beers, through its mines in

South Africa, controlled an estimated 90 percent of the world's production of rough diamonds.[14]

When I met Andy, he was working for a small consultancy company that was advising African governments but he had started his career working in De Beers. Given I too was working with various government agencies by then, I could understand and relate to the consultancy company's engagement with African governments. However, his earlier employment with De Beers was rather different, another 'kettle of fish' entirely.

He once said to me "If only we'd met years ago!" I chuckled and asked:

"So you think that if we had met when I was – in your words – wasting taxpayers' money having fun at university, generally burning my bra and stomping around Greenham Common with the Campaign for Nuclear Disarmament while you were – in my words – happily exploiting poor Africans, we would have hit it off?"

"Let me think about that for a minute."

Over the years, I would hear anecdotes of his early working life which surprised, shocked and amused in equal measure. I suggested that he wrote down those stories because they are not only interesting in themselves but they belong to a bygone era. I suspect that many people would disapprove of how he and his colleagues used to operate, but that was the situation then and I feel it would be senseless to cast aspersions through a twenty-first century lens. It was the late 1970s and what I would describe as the days of the Wild West of the diamond industry, where anything was deemed acceptable and African clients had no way of knowing what prices they could demand for their diamonds. To my mind, it is interesting to understand how and why the diamond industry changed. Andy once told me:

"In many respects, I am the last of this diamond buyer generation because the work no longer exists as I knew it. It came to an end for two main reasons: communications and education. Nowadays even the diamond digger at the bottom of a pit can call Antwerp for the latest prices, so he too has a good idea as to the value of rough diamonds."

Over the course of Andy's working life, the jobs he did and the roles he played varied enormously in line with major changes in the diamond industry. What I found most fascinating was that long before 'Human Resources' existed as a discipline and got its teeth into quasi scientific recruitment procedures, De Beers appeared to have cloned the ideal diamond buyer just as they seemed to have cloned ideal security officers. Having met some of his colleagues, it struck me that they were all of a similar background: comfortable middle-class, private schooled, fun and adventurous souls with a devil may care attitude, mostly incredibly honest and brave despite not earning high salaries. Perhaps a dash of the swashbuckling Errol Flynn without the swordplay.

How did he get into this line of work? After what he describes as a rather lacklustre academic performance at a public school where his Careers Master suggested he became a bank manager, he went to see the Public Schools Advice Bureau in London who suggested he interview with the Diamond Trading Company (DTC). The Diamond Trading Company is better known as De Beers, though in fact DTC is just one of the several companies in the De Beers Group. There was an instant point of connection for Andy with this company because his mother had been one of the many women working there sorting diamonds during the Second World War.

Andy was hired and began working in 1973 at the age of 18. He was promised a life of travel, and he reported to work for the princely salary of £1,200. Although the job was in London and everyone wore suits, it was in effect a factory line production. Diamonds bought from around the world would be acidized, sieved and sized, much of this by hand although in later years by machines. These different sizes were handed out to various departments for further sorting for colour, shape and quality, all part of the evaluation process.

Five years went by in various departments. These were the days of heavy inflation (20 per cent plus) so he felt particularly rich when his salary rose to £1,500 in the second year. Then Edward Heath, the Prime Minister at the time, called for a wage freeze so his salary did little or nothing during the following years. One year he got a 0 per cent pay rise, and a friend said "You can honestly say your pay rise isn't worth the paper it's written on!"

During this period, he spent six months in Antwerp, where he had a bedsit across from a park. One of the guys there gave him a top tip: pull the bed out of the wall (it folded up to give more space) or else you would swear someone had stolen it if you came back from a night out pissed. The DTC branch office in Antwerp was called Diamdel, and they worked closely with the diamond market there to ascertain trends and price changes. They bought diamonds in London as would any other client, and made their own assortments for their clients and thereby attempted to make money.

Andy came to hear about a buyers' training programme. This was made up of individuals whom the Company thought would be capable of buying diamonds overseas. He wasn't chosen originally so he lobbied to be included. There were about a dozen of the buyers. The Company decided that because they were to be sent to French-speaking Africa, they should attend French conversational courses. These one-on-one classes were held daily in Oxford Street from 10 -12. Andy had a girlfriend, Nicolette, who lived close by. He recounts:

"It seemed pointless to disturb the others by going to the office first, so like a cock with two plumes, I sauntered down Oxford Street at 09.45 daily. We never went back to the office till after 14.00 so you can see why we were all disliked. As work finished at 16.45, it was a day well spent."

Andy was in the first group of buyers to go overseas in January 1978. He was summoned to see one of the directors, Anthony Oppenheimer, who had just returned from Zaire (present-day Democratic Republic of Congo). After a short chat - buying diamonds wasn't mentioned - Oppenheimer asked: "Do you play tennis and water ski?" Replying that he did, Oppenheimer exclaimed "You'll have a wonderful time!

I asked him to describe his first impressions of life in Zaire.

"The tours in Zaire varied in length from five to seven months, and the trips to Kinshasa via either Paris or Brussels took approximately eight hours. Africa and its airports in those days hit you like an assault. The planes were always packed, and Africans didn't seem to have any idea of the meaning of 'one piece of hand luggage'. Everyone was in a hurry to get off for what lay ahead. There were hordes of people, general confusion, and heavy humidity.

Immigration and Customs was another term for official robbery. Everyone wanted something. No papers were ever in order: 'You have a big problem.' Happily for me and the others, we were met by our fixer, Timo, who was either related to or had already bribed all these guys, so it was smooth sailing. The Company took every opportunity to ship out as normal luggage a range of spare parts for the plane, the cars, generators, etc. Nothing was too big or heavy. You could only assume that it was faster than normal air freight; cost obviously wasn't an issue.

"I was taken into town to the flat of the Junior Administrator in Kinshasa. It was large and open plan with a wonderful view from the balcony over the city, and impressive for a young lad in his early twenties. All buyers stayed there at weekends, but this was my first night sleeping in central air conditioning. I remember commenting on the noise it made, though it was considerably quieter than the wall-mounted air conditioners we had upcountry.

The next morning, far too early, I boarded the company plane, which seated six to eight people and had two pilots, Ken and Brian. It was a Beechcraft jet prop, call sign Charlie Zulu Delta. There is a feeling I suspect you never quite get over, even if you own an aeroplane, when the pilots says to you 'Are you ready? Shall we go now?'

"But this flight wasn't only for me. It supplied the buying station with shopping and correspondence, and of course endless amounts of local cash, the Zairois currency or Zs. After brief formalities, we took off. Although it was the wet season, the skies were clear and blue. The flight to Tshikapa, about 1,000km south-east towards the Angolan border, took nearly two hours. The terrain is rolling scrub savannah with occasional settlements of mud houses with grass-thatched roofs. After a low pass over the clay rolled runway - there was no control tower - we landed.

"A Range Rover approached the plane, and Julian my boss got out. He seemed more interested in the briefcase that held the mail. There was no official interest in the plane, just the usual local Zairois, always curious. I remember that there was a smell that is difficult to describe, dry and woody. It was so silent too. As far as the eye could see, there was nothing but a heat haze and rolling bush with the occasional tree.

"At this point, it had become a custom for the chaps to take the new boy to a mud hut and say 'Just unpack, make yourself comfortable and we'll come and get you in an hour or so.'

Happily, they dropped this detour and took me directly to my house for the next six months. There were four houses in total, three in a walled compound with a swimming pool and a tennis court, and the other house, which I lived in during my second tour, was five minutes away, close to the office.

"This house had two bedrooms and a veranda, and we would sit out there in the evening enjoying a glass of whisky. There were a cook and a house boy. I shared the house with Paul, who used to become absolutely drunk out of his mind. When he lived in Liberia, the bar owner stationed someone behind Paul to catch him when he fell off his stool. I used to pick him up and drag him inside to his bedroom regularly.

"The staff for the buying station included cooks, house boys, tennis ball boys, boat boys, drivers, security, and gardeners. You name it, we had one or more to the tune of about 60 staff to serve just the five of us. The house staff had very little to do. The gardeners were forever cutting grass with a hand tool (a 'coupe-coupe') to try to keep snakes at bay. At one point, we brought over a Flymo lawnmower, which should have been perfect, but the gardener used it for two minutes before hitting a tree stump and then it was back to using the coupe-coupe.

"We took it in turns to entertain each other, and it was amazing how creative Cook could be. The staff grew vegetables, and we had guinea fowl, and avocado and papaya trees. But most of the shopping was done by placing an order with Admin in Kinshasa, which was flown up weekly. Due to massive inflation, it was best to buy big at the beginning of the tour and wind down as time progressed. The main problem was stopping Cook from helping himself to supplies of frozen chicken, steak or pork chops.

"On my first tour, there was one wife, Karen. She was tall, attractive and good company, but I suspect Steve, her husband, didn't give her the attention she wanted or needed, and six months can be a long time with nobody to talk to or confide in. She was the only white woman in a thousand kilometres if you didn't count nuns or missionaries. Sadly, their marriage ended in divorce. Was she the right woman at the wrong time? She had been one of the lads, which was a good thing; a difficult wife could be divisive in such a small isolated community.

"We were offered all sorts of creatures at the office. Steve bought Karen an African grey parrot, one of the best talkers, named CJ. He was offered a baby crocodile too, about 4 inches long with teeth like needles, but decided not to buy it. The parrot would sit on our shoulders, and we spent hours teaching it to swear. This stopped eventually as it got older. CJ continued to like Karen, but would bite us on the ears, which was quite painful.

"Nearby there was an old garage and inside were steamrollers used for levelling land, obviously newly shipped out and never used. They were coated in rust, abandoned after the Belgians left, and had numbers on the wheels and 'from Antwerp to Kinshasa'."

Diamonds in this part of Zaire were alluvial, found along river beds rather than being mined underground. The Kasai (Tshikapa) River snakes its way down from the Angolan Highlands, carrying a fortune in good quality diamonds, which are smooth and tumble along with the silt. It is unnavigable as it varies from shallows and rapids to deep and fast-running, passing unnoticed though miles of sparsely populated countryside until it joins the Zaire River and the long journey to the Atlantic.

I asked Andy to describe his job in those days. "The office was a one-storey building opposite the bank with a 'salle d'attente' (waiting room) in a gated compound. Inside the office were the four of us buyers, each stationed at a desk in front of a window. You would open your window up - one of those old casement windows which had been adapted to fold down with a metal flap - and the clients would put the diamonds on the flap, having weighed up their parcels of diamonds with coke bottle tops and matchsticks. You negotiated through an open barred window, weighed up the parcels and estimated the value of the parcel using a calculator.

"On the other side of the window was your coaxer. His job was to encourage you to pay more and for the client to accept less. Amber was an honest lad who, I believe, wanted me and the office to profit.

"One Christmas, helicopters came bringing with them new currency. There were two notes and two denominations, and as a measure against tax evasion and hoarding the Central Bank had decided to swap over the colours on the denominations. There was an announcement on the radio about this, and that no one could change more than a specified amount. Predictably, this led to chaos at the bank as people tried to exchange their money for the new currency. I saw a soldier reverse his rifle and hit a man directly on the forehead as he protested on the bank's steps. It only dazed him,

"It was an odd phenomenon that our clients didn't think there were numbers that existed above Z100,000. When this figure was reached, they would carry on negotiating for company publicity like T-shirts and baseball caps. We would maintain the charade of pretending to negotiate hard to reduce the number of company swag. Psychologically, it was important that the clients felt they had won a good deal.

"The problem with buying diamonds in Zaire at the time was the government needed dollars in the Central Bank, so they insisted that we buy in the local currency, the Zaire. The currency was essentially worthless, so transactions were made using bricks of 5 or 10 Z notes. $100,000 in the local currency would have been a mountain of bricks. With four buyers buying, we were able to go through an astonishing amount.

"The Company had its plane, Zulu Delta, flying permanently around the country to banks in the larger towns to exchange dollars for local currency. The entire cabin in the small six-seater plane with two pilots could easily be filled with bags of cash. On one occasion, I flew down with them to pick up money from Lubumbashi. The co-pilot had already crawled over the money to close the door. I was told they couldn't take off with me sitting on the toilet because the nose wheel was off the ground. I moved forward and spread-eagled myself over the bags of money with only a short gap between me and the ceiling of the plane as it took off. No fastening seat belts on this occasion. After we had taken off, the pilots told me I could resume my more comfortable seat on the toilet.

"When the diamonds were shipped, there was a local official from the Mines Department who came in to ensure that everything was weighed up and sealed. The diamonds were placed on a very big scale with weights. It was a fiddly business, I remember, putting bigger and then a number of smaller weights to make up the balance. Once we got close enough, we would call out "c'est juste" (it's correct").

"De Beers had a price book for all categories of diamonds. The prices would change once a year, sometimes up, sometimes down. But it was more difficult sitting in the office in Zaire because, don't forget, all those categories of colour are simply in your mind. It's easy enough with shape, but with colours, you have to remember the nine shades of white through to yellow. The office back in London would try to send back their immediate estimate of our results, so that we knew if we should raise or lower our prices slightly.

"I remember my first diamond purchase. It was a stone of a few carats, of reasonable white colour. The quality I remember was 'speculative', and I recall handing over the money in cash, confident only from the waist up. As time went by and my confidence grew, there were some additional negotiating skills that could be brought to bear. These weren't my ideas. If a seller asked for far too much money, then I would either slip below the bench and appear with a hideous rubber mask on my face or activate my laugh bag to the amusement of the clients in the salle d'attente with the exception of the client sitting in front of me. In negotiating, I discovered anything that broke the ice or an impasse was normally worth the effort.

"The diamonds were shipped to London, and we received individual results. It was a nerve-wracking time when they came over the radio on the open line. A company called Regideso, the national electricity company, would be communicating all day on the one frequency, and our results would have to come down the same line, so they would try to send them when the traffic wasn't so heavy.

"We all had individual code names. London underground stations I remember was one series. Results would be announced like this: Liverpool St· Donkey 3 or Jackass 3. Donkey represented a profit; Jackass a loss.

"Negotiating and buying were like a drug, and we needed it. If the exchange rate was against us or London had set high profit targets and we couldn't buy, a deep gloom descended. Lethargy was terrible. If someone suggested doing anything, they would be met with "Fuck off!" although a cocktail-making competition did get some traction. I can't for the life of me remember what was in the cocktail I made, other than that I decorated it with a frangipani flower. The sap from the stem went into the cocktail and turned our teeth black. Maybe boredom was safer?

"The number of diamond offices was strictly regulated, and the only competition in town was a company called Meltax. Competition was friendly. They were well provisioned from Libreville, so being invited to dinner was a pleasure. From time to time, London would instruct us not to talk to them, but we never took any notice. It was plain stupid. I found throughout my buying career that although we were all in competition and playing all sorts of strategic games against each other, everyone came to the rescue if something went wrong, using their influence or through the common problem solver: money."

A few years after Andy had left, the second largest stone ever was found and purchased in the Tshikapa office. It was found by a consortium of diggers. Word got out quickly and apparently the diggers quickly descended on the office for safety, even for their lives. Everyone was looking for them. The buyer who eventually bought it told Andy about the negotiation. The client had started at a price with endless zeros. The buyer started at $300,000. The plane had already been called before the purchase was finalised, and the clients hid in the bush until it arrived. The stone was sold for $5 million in the end. When cut, it became without value though estimates put it at over $100 million.

They gave the seller an option of either $5m now in cash or $1 million now with the balance held in Switzerland until the heat of the discovery had died down.

Unfortunately, he chose the first option and someone from London flew out with the full $5M. Everyone from the President down would most likely have become his 'best friends with menaces'. Andy doubts that any of the consortium members would have a penny left today.

Most of Andy's stories focused on the fun, amusement and interesting anecdotes in Zaire.

"During the week, at about midday Julian would say 'Andy get rid of your client, it's lunch.' Water skiing and lunch were next - very civilised. Life was fun. Lounging by the pool and water skiing occupied much of our free time. There is a fine photo of me skiing on the Kassai wearing nothing but a monoski.

"The river allowed for good flat-water skiing for a few miles. We were limited by a bridge that connected us with the village and shallow rapids. We even had wildlife: two hippos, a cow and a calf resided on a sand bank. We didn't appreciate just how dangerous they could be as we skied by fairly close. Of the many dangerous animals in Africa, hippos account for the most deaths among humans. Unfortunately nature was no match for the army machine guns that slaughtered them for their meat.

"The evening schedule typically involved swimming or playing tennis on our clay court. If we felt that the court was getting uneven or needed resurfacing, someone was dispatched with the pickup truck to find and bring back ant hills. Ants made these large hills of fine red soil. These were then rolled wet onto the playing surface with a roller and set hard under the baking sun. And voilà - Wimbledon! Forgetting to bring new tennis balls back from the UK was a crime. To prevent losing any, countless men were stationed around the fenced court to find and pick up any errant balls.

"At the weekend, someone would suggest a BBQ at the boat house. All the china, glasses and cold boxes were elaborately packed up. A cook and others were sent ahead to arrange everything, and we would follow leisure. Life was good and I think we appreciated the fact. The boat with boat boy was a short distance from the compound. Someone had built a Spanish-style boat house with arches by the bank of the river. He had had the lads demolish a house for the bricks. I suspect the occupants were out at the time. Anything was possible - we had the money and the manpower.

"Saturday night was film night. The Kinshasa office would send us rolls of film, and we would put out a large white sheet by the pool or project against the wall. We never had to worry about twilight. At 18.19 it was light; at 18.20 pitch dark.

"We would invite over two Mennonite missionaries who lived in Tshikapa. Herman and Ruth came from the US. They would do a five-year tour, with a year off to see family and friends, to recover from various illnesses, and raise more money so they could continue God's work.

They never looked well. Herman had a constant yellow pallor which I'm sure was a result of too many bouts of malaria. They sold gardening equipment cheaply to foster the idea of growing food. Most of this equipment was used for digging for diamonds, I'm sure.

"On our pool nights, we would offer them a fruit punch heavily laced with gin or vodka. Ruth rather liked it, but as soon as Herman realised what she was drinking he would invoke God's name and forbid it. It was sad as you could see that Ruth had lost her faith in this godless part of the world. The plane used to bring up supplies for them, and they lived for mail and word from home.

"After water skiing one day, we returned to the compound to find Herman distressed. He explained in his slow Southern American drawl that he had been 'collecting eggs from the hen house there' when a cobra spat at him, blinding him in one eye. By good luck, his glasses had taken the brunt of the venom, but Julian asked me to take him to a missionary hospital five or six miles away. I drove through the village and along mud roads with rainwater in potholes so deep that the water sloshed up to the headlights. I remember cursing the jeep, slamming the steering wheel to urge it on as if it were a horse, trying to keep it going while Herman told God that it was ok to take his sight. We arrived at the missionary hospital, where there was no light because they had no generator.

"Conveying little sense of urgency, Herman started to recount his lengthy story: 'I was collecting eggs from the hen house there...' when I interrupted him, brimming over with frustration: 'For God's sake, tell them about the snake!' Fortunately, he regained his sight.

"On other Saturdays, we sometimes went into 'town'. The village was a congregation of shacks, houses and shops. In the centre was a bar/disco called the Bim Sum where we drank Tusker beer. We'd arrive, and they would bring out high-backed chairs like thrones. It was impossible to talk as the music was so loud. You could actually feel the bass hammering on your chest. The Zairois music was wonderful for the surroundings and atmosphere.

"Julian threw a party at the Bim Sum for our clients and local dignitaries on a national holiday. The Mines representative was there along with the guy from Regideso, the head of the non-existent national electricity company. The evening went well with lots of local chop and beer. At the end of the evening, Julian had organised a lucky draw. It was rigged so he drew out numbers that corresponded with our senior guests. The Mines guy was delighted with a shovel. The electricity guy won a paraffin lamp, much to our amusement.

"The other diversion was to fly up to Kinshasa for the weekend, which was permitted every five weeks or so. This entailed leaving Friday at lunchtime and staying with the admin guy. Weekends included a certain amount of drunkenness and eating in some excellent, very expensive restaurants. The company picked up the bill for these outings.

"Sundays there were almost always spent on the Zaire/Congo River. It is an almighty force, which rises in the East African Highlands and Lake Tanganyika, and it is the deepest river in the world, 720 feet in places. It spans 2,920 miles from the Zambian border to the Atlantic, and is the ninth longest river in the world. We visited the plaque in Burundi where Stanley met Livingstone with the memorable words 'Dr Livingstone, I presume?'

"The river separates Kinshasa from Brazzaville, capital of the other Congo. Stanley left looking for the river's origin from close to where we used to have lunch (now called Stanley Pool) under the cliffs. Exploring in those days was brave stuff as the Congolese interior was challenging: tribes were hostile and disease was rife. Even today, the river is used as a highway into the interior. The Belgians did little to open up the country, and road-building in the interior is virtually non-existent. Mobuto was President for 32 years, and he did little to develop the country apart from developing mining activities from which he profited handsomely.

"Of the two seasons, everyone preferred the wet season. The sky was blue, and it was hot. Black clouds would appear, the wind would come up, and it would rain heavily for an hour until the blue skies returned. By contrast, in the dry season it was overcast all the time, and felt cold despite being virtually on the equator. In the wet season, the river level went down in Kinshasa as it was the dry season in East Africa. This exposed wonderful white sand that formed a chain of islands which, when dry, made super beaches.

"However hungover we were, we had to be at the boat club by midday or be left behind. Picnicking, playing boules, drinking, and more water skiing were usual. Sometimes we would visit our counterparts in Brazzaville. The manager brought me a 26-inch tv set when I worked in Brazzaville, which was smuggled across the river on a Sunday. Despite a full and busy weekend, I was always happy to see the meandering Kasai River from the window of Zulu Delta.

"There was an odd occasion in Tshikapa either in 1979 or 1980. We were working, when around 10am it became dark. We went outside and someone drove back to the compound with the headlights on because it was so dark. The local Zairois thought that it was the end of the world. Then the moon shifted a touch and a shaft of sunlight came through almost like a spear. I remember the feeling when everyone cheered. We had no idea that we had witnessed a total eclipse of the sun!"

To expand their ability to gather diamonds and increase profits, another buying station deeper in the country at a place called Luebo was opened. At first, Andy and his colleagues thought that Zulu Delta would take them up there in the comfort they had come to expect. The plane did a test run, but the runway was just undulating grass and it landed with the props dangerously close to the ground as it bounced along. The pilots, Ken and Brian, decided that they would not fly to Luebo unless there was a medical emergency. So trips there had to be by road. Andy described his first journey:

"It was incredibly uncomfortable. We went through villages where I don't think they had seen any white people before. The roads were soft sand, which often needed 4x4 vehicles to navigate. By early evening, I could see the new outpost in the distance all lit up as we approached. At that point, we ran out of petrol so we started to walk in pitch darkness. I tried to reassure myself that our dog Jenny would scare away any snakes.

"The next cunning plan was to make friends with the missionaries as they had a small single engine plane, and were always short of everything. Mark was the pilot. The flight was about an hour, and he navigated by compass and dead reckoning - in other words by recognising landmarks, rivers, etc. It was interesting as we flew low over the jungle canopy and were able to make out small settlements deep in the forest. Lives were being led there as they had been for centuries, harsh and unforgiving with no influence from the outside world other than paraffin lamps perhaps. When we were late arriving, Mark would ask 'Did you realise we were lost?' .....er yes.

"I spent weeks at a time in Luebo. The house and office had been commandeered. They consisted of two bedrooms, an office and a safe room, which is where I slept the first night. I awoke covered in bites. The place was surrounded by chainlink fencing. Jobs needed doing, and a pit was dug for filling toilets and showers. We had a cook, but we lived like animals behind this new shiny chain-link fence. We had radio contact with the other office, but there was no swimming pool or tennis court, and very little to do.

"I went up there with a Zairois fellow, Mali, a bit of a wide boy[15]. He was very new, and I think he was sent up there with me because it was felt he could cause less damage in Luebo. He said he could drive and he had a UK provisional license, but he reversed his car into the compound, nearly taking down the power lines in Tshikapa. Driving wasn't his strong suit.

"Our gruelling days lasted between 9 and 9.30am in Luebo. Naturally, we would want clients to come to the office. I told Mali to buy everything at the best price to attract business, even if he thought it expensive. He didn't, letting a parcel go. I had to send someone after the client to press money on him to come back.

"In the evening, I would take Jenny the dog, who was the size of a Labrador, for a walk either on the runway or in the woods. One day she ran across two stainless steel hoops sticking out of the ground, and I realised there had been a swimming pool there, long since reclaimed by the forest, dating back to at least 30 years to the Belgian colonial period.

"Mali wanted to bring a live goat back from Luebo in the car as they cost more in Tshikapa. Rather unreasonably, I told him no way. I wasn't going to sit in a car for seven or eight hours with a goat on board bleating and trying to get out! You had to be careful not to use a lot of four-wheel drive because it used up more fuel. We once ran out of fuel with tons of diamonds and a lot of money on board. Fortunately, a client was going past and he and his friend gave us a lift on the back of their Vespa to their village. They brought out big throne-like chairs for us to sit down. Not even Mali could communicate with them in their local language. The client came up with an exorbitant price for the fuel. When I protested he said 'When I'm in your office, you set the price, but out here we are in my office.' We paid up and were quickly on our way.

"Looking back, life in Tshikapa and Luebo was a great introduction to the African bush. I enjoyed the company of wonderful colleagues, other buyers, the coaxers, and the Zairois. It was sad that after a couple of tours there, I never went back."

Chapter 4: 'He who rides on the donkey does not know how hot the ground is' (Ghanaian proverb)

After leaving Guinea, my life was at a crossroads. I returned to the UK and had to decide what to do next. I did some soul searching and decided to continue doing the same sort of work I had done in Guinea, though I'm not sure if that was motivated by a sense of mission or a lack of any better idea.

I called the UK Overseas Development Administration (ODA) and asked to speak to someone who worked in the West Africa section. Surprisingly, I was put straight through to an advisor who suggested a meeting. I showed off my proudest credential: a letter of thanks from the World Bank for my services in the NGO Liaison Unit, signed by President Wolfensohn himself. The letter had impressed my former boss, who said he'd never received a thanks from any Bank president. It did not seem to impress the ODA advisor, but when I bristled and pointed out that this letter was in my view worth far more than the average reference, he laughed and admitted that it was an unusual calling card. Apparently I had contacted him at a good time, since he was looking for a social development consultant on an education project in Ghana.

In contrast to Guinea, Ghana had moved gradually, relatively peacefully, and rather hand-in-hand with the

British powers, towards independence. The ninth-century Berber historian and geographer al-Yaʿqūbī described ancient Ghana as one of the three most organised states in the region. Its rulers were renowned for their wealth in gold, the opulence of their courts, and their warrior and hunting skills. Over the centuries, several ancient kingdoms rose to eminence and were overthrown, but by the 18th century a confederacy of Ashanti states consolidated politically and militarily into the Ashanti Empire.

From the 15th century, European traders arrived in what became known as the Gold Coast: initially Portuguese, then Dutch, and later English, Swedish, and Danish. Military confrontations between the Ashanti and Fante contributed to the growth of British influence on the Gold Coast, as the Fante states—concerned about Ashanti activities—signed the Bond of 1844 that allowed the British to usurp judicial authority from African courts.

Having expanded their judicial powers, the British proclaimed the existence of the Gold Coast Colony in 1874. Though the coastal peoples were unenthusiastic, there was no popular resistance so Britain gradually acquired more control over the Ashanti areas, and a British protectorate came into existence in 1901.

British authorities adopted a system of indirect rule for colonial administration in which traditional chiefs maintained power, but took instructions from their European supervisors. It was through British-style education that a new Ghanaian elite was created, and by the end of the Second World War the Gold Coast colony was the richest and most educated of West African territories.

Independence came gradually with the electoral victory of Nkrumah's Convention People's Party (CPP) in 1951, ushering in five years of power-sharing with the British. In 1956, the new assembly passed a motion authorising the government to request independence within the British Commonwealth, which was granted the following year and lasted until Ghana declared itself a fully autonomous republic in 1960.

The 1960s to 1980s witnessed a period of economic decline, corruption, and a number of political coup d'états both successful and unsuccessful, resulting in a series of military governments. Unlike Guinea, Ghana's rulers did not descend into witch-hunting and mass arrests and executions.

Official assistance from donor countries to Ghana's recovery programme averaged US$430 million in 1987, more than double that of the preceding years. The Provisional National Defence Council (PNDC) administration also made a remarkable repayment of more than US$500 million in loan arrears dating to before 1966. In recognition of these achievements, international agencies had pledged more than US$575 million to the country's future programmes by May 1987.

However, many problems remained, including the high rate of Ghanaian unemployment as a result of the PNDC belt-tightening policies. After two years of deliberations and public hearings, district assemblies were created as local governing institutions that would offer opportunities to the ordinary person to become involved in the political process. An assembly was to become the highest political authority in each district, which was quite an advanced democratic initiative at the time. In 1992, there were multi-party elections and a return to democracy.

This was the country I first visited in 1995, a nation of largely confident, self-assured people who seemed at ease in their relationship with Britain. It was also a country where, in contrast to Guinea, donor aid was substantial, a situation that was immediately obvious in the education sector where I worked.

The ODA education programme was run out of an Education Field Office managed by one Howard Tyers, a former teacher and a friendly and mild-mannered man keen for his team to work constructively together. His teaching ethic was deeply inculcated, and he gave me an excellent understanding of the programme and insight as to what I should do to carry out my tasks. His team included some advisors - civil servants from ODA - who would arrive on short-term visits, supported by independent consultants. I had easy and direct communication with all of them, and we often travelled together to schools to maximise synergy in our findings. In the capital, Accra, we would all stay at the same hotel and discuss our work until late at night. At weekends he would occasionally invite a few of us out to lunch. Years later, I would realise that this was an extraordinarily collegiate and beneficial working relationship, which unfortunately did not extend to his colleagues for many more years.

Now, having previously carved up Africa, the donor agencies were engaged in carving up parts of the education sector and geographical areas of the country. The government had prioritised an ambitious policy, known as FCUBE (free, compulsory, universal basic education), which required a lot of additional funding.

The World Bank was a big player in education, along with several so-called bilateral donors, individual countries such as the UK, which funded aid. Each of them had their own offices and at times separate education programme offices. The Ministry of Education would become so bogged down in meeting requests from all these agencies that its senior staff appointed individuals to act as buffers against the donors so that they could get on with their jobs. With so many donor projects and programmes, Ministry staff were constantly requested to provide information and views, accompany donor staff on their visits to schools, and take part in the endless rounds of project and sector quarterly and annual reviews and evaluations.

We consultants produced a lot of lengthy reports too, which were sent to dozens of people in the UK ODA and the Ghana education service. A friend once dared me to insert a spurious word, 'jollification', into some of my reports as a way of checking if anyone ever read them. I passed the dare onto another friend who was a management consultant and whose reports were even less likely to touch on this improbable subject than my own, and he rose to the challenge. Only one of his colleagues ever asked him about the peculiar word in one of his reports.

Ghana became like a science lab under a microscope with all the education projects. Many donors focused on building schools, but even here the quality, standards, and cost of these schools varied enormously, the Japanese being the outliers. Their schools cost at least three times more than anyone else's, because they were required by Japanese law to lay anti-seismic foundations despite the fact that Ghana was not prone to earthquakes. The Americans, I was informed, took on one or two districts and proceeded to graft all-American systems and structures onto schools, no expense spared.

With all this duplication, incoherence and the high transaction costs imposed on Ministry staff, it is probably hardly surprising that a later British Secretary of State, Clare Short, by then Secretary for International Development, pushed to drop all these separate projects and replace them with 'sector support'. This entailed working within the ministries' own systems, providing a combination of direct budget support and technical assistance to build or improve their structures, training, and operating systems. The understanding was that if we agreed with the Ministry's overall policy thrust, we would support them to achieve it rather than set up parallel systems.

My job was to advise on how to get more girls to attend and stay in school. The terminology was 'improving access to education', and accompanied by an array of donor terms including 'equity' and 'gender'. This meant I had to visit schools, talk with teachers, parents, and influential people such as local chiefs to ask them why children did not attend or dropped out of school. Fortunately, Howard saw fit to provide me with a comfortable vehicle and safe driver on what proved to be many long journeys.

The World Bank had put up structures in most schools, which for some reason they named rather grandly 'pavilions', but these were simply the basic frame and roof of a building. The agreement with the Ministry was that local communities would then do their bit and clad the walls to take ownership of the structures, however we often discovered on school visits that the walls had not yet been clad.

On later visits, when our project started an initiative to have "school improvement plans" with small budgets, a common activity selected supposedly after widespread local consultation was building football pitches. The reason given was that the Bank's pavilions had generally been constructed on the only available flat ground near the school, which was typically the football field.

It was interesting to enquire innocently how the football fields might address girls' access to schools. At times there was some squirming before the reply came that the girls would watch and cheer the matches, and then wash and repair the boys' football jerseys. Needless to say, girls did not play football at that time. Once again, I hear Andy's persistent voice in my ear in response to this finding "Quite right too, another brilliant example of a successful aid project!" Or as one parent said "I don't know if school will teach my son anything useful, but if he gets onto the Ghanaian football team, he will be made for life."

In between visits to schools, I would work with the Director and Deputy Director of the Basic Education Department back in Accra. The Director, whom her Deputy called Auntie Flo (for Florence), was among the few women at the time in such a senior position. She had been much loved in her previous job as a District Director of Education. Despite or maybe because of having no children of her own, she used to take young women teachers under her wing and mentor them.

Her secretarial office was often packed with women teachers who had come to see her. I am sure now that their concerns were what she considered her real job, but having all of us foreigners expecting to work with her on our latest development fad, she used to have to give us precedence. In any case, I suspect she more or less slept in her office so that she could do our bidding as well as her proper job. The Deputy, Auntie Mary, was a typical Ghanaian in her devout Christianity. She would have preferred to leave all our planning arrangements to God were it not for Auntie Flo's gentle suggestion that perhaps God needed a helping hand.

There was one diligent man, Daniel, who worked in a small department not captured in any aid programme. With all the foreign programmes carving up the districts and parts of the education system, there were always a few departments that no one ever saw fit to include, and these were usually dusty rooms with very little furniture and several broken-down bits of old machinery or shelving.

I was told I should talk to Daniel, and he was delighted that someone was prepared to listen to his Big Idea for education. In effect, Daniel was ahead of his time because he had devised a system which now looks to me like school league tables in the UK. In one district, he had introduced a special maths and English exam to test all levels of primary school children. The results were then displayed in a table, ranking all the schools in that district, and each school had to show and discuss the results in a community and parents meeting. A few years into his experiment, he had already found that parents were pressurising teachers to improve their teaching performance, and that the low performers were generally moving up the league table. For some reason, no donor had thought to try to replicate this idea.

On one occasion, three of us spent a week in the cocoa-growing area in Ghana, a town called Sefwi Wiawso, to learn about the impact of an earlier school initiative. My street credibility during subsequent meetings with Ministry staff was the fact that I had spent a week in this rather remote town and that I could actually pronounce it correctly (it sounds more like Sechwee Yoso). We visited schools, and talked to local communities about their schools, and we were almost hallucinating with hunger throughout the week. Despite the vast expanse of cocoa plants, there was very little fresh food, and when our Ghanaian driver said that he himself did not trust the cleanliness of food preparation, we too felt wary. "Let them eat chocolate" (*pace* Marie Antoinette) was not even an option: the raw cocoa beans have a particularly bitter taste and can cause a serious stomach upset.

Inspecting the number of text books in one school, I had intended to ask if they had enough per pupil, but found myself asking if the school had enough food. I hastened to correct myself. At the end of the week, we had a meeting at the home of the District Director of Education. We sat down in his comfortable living room, and on the coffee table there was huge hand of bananas. I started to give my speech, but after a few introductory sentences I couldn't resist pausing, despite feeling an idiot, to ask the Director if we could help ourselves to a banana. He chuckled and said of course; he'd heard that we had been looking for bananas during our visit and had had them brought expressly for us.

During the lengthy journey to and from Sefwi Wiawso, we talked about Ghanaian customs and habits. A Canadian, Lesley, had married into the Casely-Hayford family, one of whom had been a prominent supporter of pan-African nationalism. Lesley explained to me the social importance of funerals. Up till then, I'd been a bit dismissive of a people who appeared on the surface to invest more in the dead than the living, but in a country where working people do not take holidays, funerals are an important opportunity to meet up with the wider family and clan, to arrange business deals, find marriageable partners for young family members, and so on.

That said, Lesley admitted that there were Ghanaians who found it reprehensible that while many a family never had money for medical care, there was always enough for an elaborate funeral. On one occasion, the dead man actually attended his own lavish funeral. The story behind his surprising appearance was that he had been ill, and his doctor had grown exasperated over the family's apparent inability to cover the cost of medical treatment. As a result, the family were informed that their father/husband had died. However, the doctor himself had secretly paid for the man's treatment so he survived. The aim of his appearance at the funeral wake was to shame the family over their questionable priorities. Instead, they were furious with the doctor for tricking them.

One day, the local newspaper ran the headline "Can cotton grow rice?" This seemingly innocent title covered a huge scandal and moral outrage. An elusive black American woman called Miss Cotton had travelled to Ghana, where she proceeded to carry out a sting operation. She persuaded President Kufuor to meet her under the full glare of the media, and accept her grain company's offer of ten bags of rice with a view to winning a rice production contract. Her 'success' (not without a certain innuendo regarding Miss Cotton's relationship with the President) was later announced by the Attorney General and Ministers of Justice and Agriculture, who slammed the previous government for guaranteeing a loan running to several million dollars to a company that existed only in name.

To add insult to injury, someone had made a copy of Miss Cotton's wedding ceremony back in her Baptist Church in America, which was taken back to Ghana. During the singing and speeches, Miss Cotton proclaimed "The Lord said ask and thou shalt be given. I asked and I was given! Praise the Lord!" The moral outrage of this woman's perverted sense of religion can only be imagined among Ghana's deeply Christian community.

Thanks to close collaboration with my colleagues, I asked one day if I could accompany the the Department for International Development (DFID) Teacher Advisor to visit a teacher training college. The visit fell outside my narrow remit, but I was curious to see the conditions students studied under. It was an eye-opener to discover a modern, very well built, designed, and equipped college with what looked to me like fairly rigorous classes underway. Teachers and students alike were smartly dressed, and it was clear that they considered themselves part of an important if not elite occupational group.

I addressed a class of about 30 male and female students and asked them, in the light of their government's education policy, whether any of them were interested or willing to take up jobs in the more remote rural schools where there were chronic shortages of teachers. Only one student put up his hand, and even he said cautiously that he would be prepared to go to a rural school for just a few years. A common theme among the views of the other students was that their parents had made huge sacrifices for them to become teachers, and they wanted to repay them by getting jobs in the more prestigious schools in towns where they could settle, and where their future children could in turn benefit from a good education.

It was disappointing, but not too surprising, to discover a few years down the line in 2003 during an evaluation of this education programme, that the vast increase in school enrolments over the period had taken place within the private education sector, which educated about one in five of all school children. These private schools had shown an increase of around 50 per cent in primary and 100 per cent in junior secondary, while enrolment in public schools had barely increased by just three and two per cent in these categories.

Private schools were usually based in towns, and a key factor in their superior results was said to be better management of teachers to ensure their attendance and proper teaching. Some of these schools were religious, others not, and mostly fees were nothing like as exorbitant as one would expect in Europe, but nevertheless they were not free.

While the donors had concentrated on handing public school teachers "carrots" – state-of-the-art teacher training colleges, incentives to work in rural areas, etc. – they had not paid attention to "sticks" – disciplinary measures. In the end it seemed Ghanaian parents, many of whom were not at all wealthy, voted to make further sacrifices to ensure their children got a decent education. The end of programme report (1998 to 2002) noted merely that the growth of private schools posed 'challenging' issues of quality and access in public schooling. This was a perfect example of civil service understatement. I thought back to Daniel, sitting in his dusty office in the Ghana Ministry of Education, writing up by hand the latest results of his league tables for comparing school performance in districts. His experiment should have been taken up and spread across the country.

A Ghanaian friend once quoted a proverb to me: "He who rides on the donkey does not know how hot the ground is." What do we foreigners really understand about Ghanaian culture and values, and in particular how much Ghanaians value education? We are not walking on the hot ground.

What struck me was the contrast between the education projects in Guinea and Ghana – they were chalk and cheese. Guinea with its few donor agencies and committed individuals had achieved hugely impressive results in education while Ghana awash with donor projects in education had produced highly unimpressive results.

When I was working later as an advisor in DFID, an email went around asking for examples of education programmes' results with a view to touting some success stories. I wrote back with an outline of the Ghana education programme and its rather chequered results. No one responded to my email.

Chapter 5: Landmines and urban project in Angola

Thanks to my fairly fluent Portuguese after living in Mozambique, I won a new assignment with DFID around 1997 to make a short visit to Angola along with a military expert to update the British government's strategy on landmines. The purpose of this mission was rather convoluted and probably completely useless, not to mention fairly dangerous for me. It was Princess Diana's concern over landmine victims that had guilt-tripped the UK government into needing to claim it was doing something, a bit like all those commissions set up to investigate various matters which shock or anger the public. The commissions report many years later and certainly well after the original outrage has died down so that their wishy-washy recommendations go unnoticed.

While she was in Angola, Princess Diana visited many child victims of landmines in the constant and visible company of the British Red Cross, who ensured her visit was highly televised. On one occasion, she was fully kitted up in protective clothing and shielding to walk through an area supposedly just cleared of landmines, and talk with people removing mines.

"They probably got a long line of black guys to walk back and forth and thereby 'clear' the entire area first," Andy suggested later.

"It wouldn't surprise me. How would it have looked if the future queen of England – as she was then – had been disabled or killed in her pursuit of assisting landmine victims in far-flung Angola?"

Angola was founded in 1575 as a Portuguese colony, and remained so until 1975 after a coup d'état in Portugal the preceding year. It soon became a key country in the proxy Cold Wars fought in Africa, with the main ruling party, the MPLA, supported by the Soviet Union and Cuba, while the main rebel group, UNITA, had clandestine American and South African backing. Both groups engaged in an armed struggle that led the country into a prolonged civil war lasting until mid-1991.

It was estimated that by 1988, Cuba had around 55,000 troops in Angola, a fact which actually worried the Soviet Union as well as America. Ironically, throughout the 1980s, the Cuban Special Forces actually protected American oil infrastructure in the enclave of Cabinda - the government needed the revenue too much to be politically correct. A peace agreement was reached, and presidential and parliamentary elections were held in September 1992, but the results were contested by UNITA. Efforts to find a peaceful solution failed, and the struggle resumed, reaching unprecedented levels and devastating the country.

Angola's economy suffered enormously from the decades of war. In 1973, it was exporting oil and was the fourth-largest producer of diamonds, an important producer of iron ore, and a net exporter of food crops. But despite the increase in oil and diamond production, by the late 1990s public spending exceeded revenue and was primarily allocated to the military and security, while budget allocation on health and education was small and declining. The under-five mortality rate was the third highest in the world. The country had a huge number of landmines and one report estimated that as many as 70 people died each day through death from landmines.

Our brief in London was to find out what was being done about helping to remove landmines and report back with some recommendations, but our approach had to be low-key and on no account should the Red Cross learn of our visit. We were told quite clearly "if you see their vehicles, go off and hide." The concern was that if we spoke to Red Cross staff, we would be thrust into the media spotlight and asked awkward questions about what the UK government was intending to do. Clare Short was at the helm, and she did not want pesky, crusading charities pressurising her department to "do something" in a country where she had no desire to provide aid. Angola was already an emerging oil-producing country, and although there was a lot of poverty she saw no reason for British aid. It was not even a former British colony which might have some claim on our sense of colonial guilt. At some point, I heard that the South African government had sent the Angolan government a map of where their soldiers had laid landmines[16], which the Angolan government had rather casually misplaced. This did not exactly suggest a caring government.

One of the UK advisors was particularly keen for me to investigate the potential for local communities to be trained to remove landmines themselves, so that even in the absence of funding for experts such as Halo Trust, they could sustainably make their land safe for farming and for local children. This was a well-meaning idea which we tossed about, but I think that the de-mining experts had concerns over transferring their skills to a few selected persons in local communities in case they got themselves and others blown up. I can see today that it would have had liability written all over it. An additional problem was that in areas as yet unmined and cordoned off with metal fencing, the fencing was often removed and used for other purposes such as farming or construction.

I was told I should talk to Angolans while they were removing landmines, but no one offered me any safety kit. I was told I should take a particular route across a field which had already been de-mined to approach the men at work. About four of them, wearing heavily protective equipment, were on their knees close to each other, painstakingly combing the ground in front of them.

After the visit, I read the Halo Trust report which stated that the clearance of landmine operations was not completely successful because landmines can move. They are placed just a few centimetres below the ground precisely so that they will blow up if trodden on, but this also means that if they are on any degree of slope, heavy rain can remove both topsoil and landmines into areas which are supposedly cleared. No one had seen fit to point this out to me.

I also wondered what value had been added by my asking these men a few questions. They could only talk to me about the nature of their job, and there was no way that I would learn anything of value or importance. It seemed rather like the war correspondents who venture ever closer to the front line even when there are now other means of seeing and proving what happens on the ground. It impresses some people, and I think it may excite the correspondents themselves, but I felt no excitement and was not prepared to risk losing limb or life in order to tick a box in a report that was never meant to prompt any action.

Shortly after my Angolan landmines visit, the Department for International Development's - Great Lakes and Horn of Africa section (known to insiders as the Basket Case Countries) came up with a small project to provide highly focused support to Angola's poorest citizens. It managed to circumvent Clare Short's opprobrium of the Angolan government because none of the funding went through the government, while not quite satisfying her suspicion of NGOs, which were to be funded directly.

The project focused on alleviating urban poverty in the capital, Luanda. Luanda had became one of the most heavily populated African capitals as people gradually fled the war and poverty in the countryside. The total country population was thought to be about 15 million at the time, of whom around half had been displaced, and moved from insecure rural areas to towns and cities. Over three million had settled in peri-urban areas in Luanda alone.

I became DFID's Field Manager in 1999, a part-time job which took me to the capital, Luanda, for two weeks every quarter for the next four years.

The city of Luanda presents a curious mix of styles and socio-economic groupings. If you were to go there after South Africa or any other Southern African country which had been colonised by the British where you saw the visible geographic effects of both formal and informal apartheid, you would be struck by the absence of a race divide. The original Portuguese settlers and soldiers had had no problem with mixing with local women. People of varying shades of brown, rich and poor, rubbed shoulders as they lived side by side.

On one occasion, an irate general wrote to the director of the ministry responsible for social welfare, demanding that the street children who were squatting next door to his house be removed. A rather brave woman director wrote a polite response back to the 'Excelentissimo General', in which she firmly pointed out that the children had every right to live there, and that unless he and his men stopped waging war there would continue to be even more of them.

Luanda had a particular eclectic architectural style. Many houses had been built in a distinctly Portuguese style (asymmetrical structures with strangely curved walls) in Luanda, and a massive fortress on the hill. There was one small street just off the seafront which looked exactly like a street in Lisbon with old residential buildings, stylish restaurants, and bars. The embassy area of the city was up on a plateau which looked out to sea in the far distance, while just below sprawled one of the largest markets in Africa, where it was said that you could buy anything from food to diamonds to Kalashnikovs.

The most attractive and largest old colonial buildings housed the post office, several government offices and, grandest of all, the national bank, which had a curved frontage with an impressive entrance and a vast marble floor beyond which there was a spiral staircase. One building, constructed by Frenchman Gustave Eiffel, ended up by chance in Luanda. The story went that the building was being shipped somewhere from France, but got offloaded by accident in Luanda, and was subsequently abandoned so the Angolans eventually found a place for it.

There were few options for accommodation, aside from the two or three poor but very expensive hotels. As a nation in the midst of civil war, Angola was one of the most expensive countries in the world, which may seem counter-intuitive. However, it was largely oil, diamond, and embassy staff who went to Luanda, and none of them were paying for their own accommodation. At that time the business class British Airways flight from London to Luanda was the most expensive in the world mile for mile and always fully booked. The UK government was prepared to pay for me to fly a less expensive but longer route, which is what I did, and that gave me the scope to stop off sometimes and visit friends or colleagues in South Africa.

"Well it was fine for you, you were paid to fly business class thanks to British taxpayers," Andy used to say to me.

"Is that a touch of sour grapes from the man who used to fly first class but now has to elbow others out of the toilet seat at the back of the plane?" was my rejoinder.

After initially staying in the rundown Hotel Continental, I moved to a small guest house, called the Hospederia Soleme, run by two Angolan sisters who were charming, courteous, and knowledgeable about the country. One of them had set up a NGO some years back, and a brother was an ambassador who would drop in occasionally. Their old house had beautiful décor and high ceilings, pretty bedrooms, but - just a small downside - the communal use of the family bathroom. The sisters were excellent cooks and everyone, family and guests, ate together in their small dining room. The timing of my visits meant that I spent four birthdays in Luanda, and the sisters produced the most fabulous, moist, birthday fruit cake on each occasion.

The routine of my visits involved visiting each of the projects, discussing their quarterly reports with them, and then going to the sites of their projects to see the works and meet the people. The projects covered water, sanitation, micro-finance, and children's welfare. At that time, Angola attracted very little aid and few NGOs, partly because the Angolan government controlled the presence of foreign organisations tightly, and insisted that they work closely with government departments.

One of the NGO representatives, Dr Mary Daly, was an Irishwoman and the dynamic Co-Director of Development Workshop, the local branch of a Canadian NGO. Development Workshop was for many years the only NGO in Angola, having been set up in 1981 to provide support to the ministry responsible for urbanisation. By the end of the 1980s, Angolan associations and NGOs had been legalised and there were fewer controls on foreign NGOs.

Mary had arrived in Angola many years before to work as a doctor, but she switched to working in water and sanitation when she realised that most diseases she was presented with were easily preventable by better water and sanitation. I guess it was she, rather than the rather quiet Canadian director, who decided that the NGO should focus all its time, resources, and staff to running projects rather than have anything to do with the administration, communications or fundraising aspects. Those functions were carried out by a small British partner NGO called One World Action, which achieved a lot on a low budget. Development Workshop's offices were incredibly cramped, with one person's desk located under the stairs, and Mary herself shared an office with a couple of other staff. The meeting space was really just the hallway, and the whole office of 20 or so staff shared one tiny toilet.

Mary was a rich source of stories dating back to 1973 about the early socialist years of the independent Angolan state. An early socialist-style planning initiative had been to improve the nutrition of Angolan citizens. Eggs were an excellent source of nutrition. A calculation was made: x number of citizens times one egg per day times 365 days. The total was ordered as a one-off shipment, and the country was completely swamped in eggs. Although it is said that Angolans became quite ingenious in finding new ways to cook and preserve eggs, there was still colossal waste and one could truly say that the government was left with egg on its face.

Although I was there to monitor how well the projects were doing and give advice if necessary, I suspect I learnt more from Mary than vice versa. Unlike many NGOs in Africa, which typically campaign for free water for poor communities – a position also taken by posturing populist politicians prior to elections – Development Workshop argued that communities should pay a small fee. They had learnt that so-called free water was just free water for a few weeks, and then communities went back to paying exorbitant sums for water trucked into poor settlements by tankers. Ironically, it turned out that these communities ended up spending several hundred times more for their water than the oil company Total, located in a massive downtown office block under which street children scratched around for shelter.

Development Workshop's approach was to dig boreholes after they had got the local communities to agree to paying a small fee for every bucket of water, which would be used to cover the maintenance costs of the well and give a small fee to the water company as an incentive to maintain the water supply to the area. A water committee had to be formed among members of the community to monitor the funds and repairs as part of the deal between NGO and community. There was a triangular relationship between the water company, EPAL, local government, and the water committees. Over the years, this model was gradually refined to ensure an adequate quantity and quality of water, transparent accounting, and oversight.

Again unlike many NGOs, Development Workshop – recognised that among these poorer peri-urban families who had escaped from war, there was no real sense of community and there were unequal power relationships. Some individuals sought to gain power over others by making illegal connections to the water system. The NGO trained the water committees and local governments to deal with conflict. Payment for the service encouraged users to seek leverage against those who abused the rules. However, this was not the same as privatisation of the water system, which was also widely touted by donors in many countries. Under privatisation, a private contractor would provide the service for profit and the local government would supposedly regulate fees charged and water quality. Given the very weak state of local government, nobody would trust their ability to act as a regulator.

Mary and her team had become very pragmatic over the years. The salaries of public servants in the '90s were not worth the paper they were written on, so Development Workshop would acquire funding and hire the officials to do their own job. The standpipe water project in Luanda was done by paying the water company crews to do the work. The company director was paid costs and benefits for supervision.

Mary said "The water company's two cars with four wheel drive were maintained by our project. We paid for fuel and we paid daily allowances for certain types of work. When there was an outbreak of cholera, Development Workshop bought pickups for the Health Office in Luanda. The director of the Provincial Health Office asked me to keep the cars in the NGO's name. Every time somebody higher up in the hierarchy asked him for a car, he apologised and said he could not cede the car because it belonged to Development Workshop."

Paying public servants to do their job would have been frowned upon elsewhere due to the desire to maintain the myth that public servants were adequately paid. With such a weak public administration in Angola and few donors around to be judgemental about paying and supporting government officials, no one cried foul. Their biggest success was working with the National Director of Water. They were able to influence his drafting of the national water policy, which promoted the Development Workshop water and sanitation model.

I asked Mary what she felt was a key ingredient to her NGO's success, and she told me "The difference between us and foreign or local NGOs set up by the political elite is that we were a completely mixed ethnic group. We had the ability as an organisation to recruit Angolans who could do the job irrespective of their ethnic backgrounds. Most other NGOs would bring in one Angolan and then recruit more from their own ethnic group.

"The international staff were clued in enough to try to figure out a local perspective, for instance, how to get drinking water. We would ask how it had worked before the war, and how it could be done now. Andrew, a colleague, once told me 'We are having trouble in a *bairro* (local community) as they won't dig drains to put in the pipes.' So we went off and spoke to the movers and shakers in the *bairro*. In Angola, if you ask the question properly, they will answer it. The answer was obvious: 'We keep being asked to dig trenches and no one brings pipes. So bring the pipes first and then we'll dig the trenches!'"

Micro-finance was the other main area of the project. Variously called micro-finance or micro-credit, it is one of the widely acknowledged success stories of international development, first practised on a large scale in Bangladesh by the Grameen Bank. Poor people cannot get a bank loan because they have no collateral, therefore no asset which could be taken by the bank in the event of a default on their loan payments. There is a similar problem throughout the world, where poorer people often have to resort to infamous payday loan schemes, typically resulting in their becoming heavily indebted.

But one advantage in many poorer countries is the power of the community which acts as collateral. People have wide extended families - they know and support their neighbours, and many women in particular used group savings schemes long before aid programmes arrived. Micro-finance loans are granted to individuals in groups, so if one member defaults, the others have to cover their loan repayments. Given they know where each other lives, they can either apply support or pressure to ensure all members repay the loans. These schemes are often run alongside training on setting up and running microbusinesses.

The additional challenge in the Angolan environment was hyperinflation, which averaged 370 per cent from 1991 to 2021. In 1993, it had actually reached a peak of

1,838 per cent. However, the amazing thing was that the groups, especially women who traded on the open market, not only repaid the initial loans but went on to receive larger loans. This was a great example of local people knowing more than the so-called aid experts.

At one point, the DFID Micro-Finance Advisor came to Angola to discover how the women managed this remarkable feat. He discovered that as soon as the women received their loan in dollars, they exchanged the dollars for the local currency, the kwanza, and went to buy food. As soon as the food was sold, they exchanged kwanzas back into dollars. The currency exchanges happened once or twice a day. The important thing was to end each day with dollars in their hands, ready to change into kwanzas to purchase afresh the following day.

Development Workshop suggested I spend a few extra days of my own time in the city of Huambo to learn how they operated there. Fortunately, someone warned me about the plane journey: flying over UNITA rebel-held areas, missiles were sometimes launched at aircraft, so the pilots descended in a corkscrew formation to try to avoid being hit, which would have been rather unnerving had I not known.

I visited the local prison, where a few years earlier many prisoners had died from diseases related to poor food, hygiene, and sanitation. An aid organisation had worked closely with the prison authorities and local communities to turn around conditions in the prison and make it possibly one of the most enlightened and advanced anywhere in the world. Development Workshop provided food for work.

The prison was clean, and many prisoners were busy tending their own vegetables and fruit in a garden outside the walls. Some attended a school just outside the prison together with children from the local community. Teachers and parents had no problem with their children mixing with prisoners, though I believe none had committed violent crimes. On our return, we were asked to give one of the prisoners a lift into town so that he could purchase things for the garden. There had been no cases of prisoners trying to escape, possibly because the improved prison conditions were better than in their home villages and towns.

When I was not working, I was partying in the evenings and at weekends. With most oil company and the few diamond employees being male, this was a great place to be a single young woman. A common meeting point was the Viking Club, and seeing people there in the evenings mid-week would usually result in invitations to parties, clubs, and beach trips at the weekend.

I met an Australian helicopter pilot, Mark, who ferried people on and off the offshore oil rigs by day, and partied the rest of the time. One evening we went for dinner to the house of his American friend, who showed us a long video of his daughter's graduation ceremony, and waxed lyrically about how much he loved her and his wife. After dinner, we went on to a club where he chatted up two very young Angolan girls and took both home with him for the night.

This was by no means the first time I had come across generally older white men carrying on relationships with far younger African women. Whether they choose to acknowledge it or not, there is a huge imbalance of power between a relatively wealthy white man and a poor, young African woman. The men can exploit this power differential in a way that they would not be able to do back in Europe or North America, where they would seldom be able to attract women half their age or less. These same men apparently see no contradiction in having a very young girlfriend while supporting the country's development. It always made me feel uncomfortable.

Angola is where Andy and my paths crossed for a second time but this story comes later in the diamond tales.

Chapter 6: Brazzaville - "We don't know any Andrew Ward"

After Andy left Zaire, his next buying assignment for the Diamond Trading Company in the De Beers group took him across the Congo river to the small country of Congo-Brazzaville also known as the Republic of the Congo. It was 1979, and the Wild West of the diamond world still reigned largely unabashed and unregulated.

There were no diamonds in Congo-Brazzaville. Nevertheless at the age of 24 Andy was running a small office in Brazzaville where they shipped up to a million dollars of diamonds weekly, sometimes with a gross weight of 80kg. The Congolese benefited from exports of diamonds smuggled in from Zaire. The Zairois clients wanted payment in dollars, which they received in Congo-Brazzaville. The diamond parcels were considerably bigger in Brazzaville than they had been in Zaire (Tshikapa) - they were thousands of carats. Competition in Brazzaville was not controlled. There were two major competitors, but the rest were small fry.

Apparently, De Beers had a contractual agreement with Zaire, so every month the company would buy the diamonds mined in Miba, in Lubumbashi near the border with Zambia, which produced thousands of carats of diamonds of all sorts, but predominantly industrial grade. The average price of the industrial production was less than $20 a carat. There was a huge amount of theft every month, which ended up in Brazzaville or Bujumbura (Burundi).

Technically when Andy worked in Brazzaville or Burundi, he wasn't working for De Beers because had he done so, it would have looked as if De Beers were encouraging the smuggling. De Beers could say to President Mobutu of Zaire with plausible deniability "We don't know anyone by the name of Andrew Ward."

Instead, Andy and his colleagues worked for a Jewish man, a Mr Glatt, who was their Mr Fix It. They first met him in Brussels, where he was carrying an airline bag, which he virtually threw at them. Andy imagined he was glad to be rid of the $500,000 cash inside. Throughout the flight to Brazzaville, they kept checking that the bag was still in the overhead locker. They would send money to Mr Glatt, and he would send it on to London. But they were paid the same salary, whether they worked for Mr Glatt or De Beers.

I asked Andy to describe his life of buying diamonds in Brazzaville.

"For some reason, the buying office in Congo-Brazzaville had been closed briefly, and now it was decided that I and another chap, Jim, should re-open it. Jim had been there before, but was junior to me. Not that these things matter, but if something goes wrong, you need to know who is ultimately to blame. Later, Steve and Clive worked with me there. Clive always wore a powder blue safari suit, while we wore jeans and a T-shirt. Steve and I would wake up hungover in the morning, but Clive would come bounding out enthusiastically.

"The house and office were located under one roof in a bungalow next to the railway. The whole building shook whenever a train went by carrying lumber to the port. There was nothing grand about this place: it was situated on the road at a T-junction leading to the ferry and port. The advantage of the location was, I suppose, that all clients had to pass our office as they entered town. The Presidential Palace was a kilometre away so there was a police and army presence, which was not always a good thing.

"There were three buyers, Steve, Clive and me. Our staff numbered four. Giaome took care of the house. He cooked lunch, but we always went out at night. We had two security guards, and a general chap whose name I forget.

"The office had previously been run with just one buyer, but the pressure on that one person was enormous. Having the office and house under one roof, the clients would turn up any time of the day and night. There was a regular ferry service between Kinshasa and Brazzaville, and upon arrival their first priority was to seek out a safe place to park their diamonds. We didn't even weigh the parcels they brought in, which were heavily packaged and sealed. We would put them straight in the safe, and then we'd weigh them when they came back to negotiate. They trusted us, but they were impatient.

"Once when there had been just one person in the office, an Embassy official had contacted De Beers and said 'You ought to come and get your man, because he's going off the rails.' The pressure gets too much. You've got to be able to say to the clients 'Look, take your diamonds and fuck off.' That guy obviously couldn't. But if there are two or three of you, you back each other up. It happened to a couple of people working alone and they had to go back to England. The story was that they had to drug one guy to get him on the plane, and he woke up back in London."

This story sounded almost identical to Bob's about the De Beers man in Guinea who had gone crazy and had to be sent back to London. Fun as it may be at times, the life of a diamond buyer was apparently not for everyone. I asked Andy how they would value the huge quantities of diamond parcels in that office.

"First off, when you get a parcel you separate it all out in front of the client. You sieve it to separate the sizes. Then with the bigger ones over a carat, you look at them and size them individually. For the 'smalls' you would take a cut off, value that pile and come up with a price. The idea was to get a representative sample. To save time and pointless negotiation, I would offer the maximum market price with single stones, and if the clients didn't like it I would say 'Fine, don't accept my money. Go see Eli, my competitor. If he offers a penny more, take the money. If not, come back and I will honour my offer.' But I wasn't obliged to do so once they had left the office.

"I remember Clive used to spend hours picking up individual stones in front of the client, arguing all the time with him while he came up with enormously complex calculations. I'd look over at his calculator and see he'd already got his client below the price that he wanted to pay, so I'd say 'Pay him, Clive, pay him the fucking money!'

'But Clive would insist 'Non, non, diminuez fort!' (no, no, bring your price down!). I'd say "When the client came in here, he was clean-shaven, and now he's got a beard. Let him leave and bring back more another day.'

"It used to drive us crazy. You've got to lump things together - that's how you move along. Industrial parcels would come over in kitbags weighing literally thousands of carats. I used to have a baby bath down by the side of my chair. I would never work through these kitbags to come up with a value, I would just argue. When purchased, as was always the case, I would mix them into my baby bath stock with a running total of carats and price paid. We always made 20 per cent profit.

"Despite there being three of us buyers, the pressure was still on. I used to drink gallons of coffee and become quite aggressive with the clients. My boss once insisted I give up coffee, which I did, only to suffer blistering headaches. We would get a phone call from London occasionally asking us to do something, but I'd ignore it. I'd start making a hissing static sound and say 'I can't hear you, are you there?' and then put down the phone. In one sense, those in charge understood the problems we were facing well enough as they had previously done our job, but maybe on a wet November day back in London they would have forgotten about those pressures.

"I loved the job in Brazzaville. For the first time, I was in charge and I had a lot of responsibility for buying and the security of the office. It was exhilarating to be engaging with very smart clients from Senegal and Zaire.

"These clients were Muslims who prayed five times a day, so it wasn't unusual to have our driveway covered with men in splendid attire of all colours on their knees, praying in the direction of Mecca. During the month of Ramadan, when they were required to fast during sun-up, we took great delight in munching a variety of biscuits and fruit throughout the day whilst negotiating. They could be tough people to negotiate with, and life is full of small victories. Age commands respect in Africa, so at just 24 years and despite buying more than anyone else in town, respect for us was in short supply."

In contrast to the diamond diggers in the Zairois bush, Andy's Congolese clients in Brazzaville were a different breed. There was a hierarchy of diamond dealers from the digger at the bottom of the pit to the men who had bought the concessions to diamond collectors or tradespeople who would gather larger quantities of stones and take them to Kinshasa or across the river to Brazzaville. Andy would meet those at the top of this hierarchy for the most part, who had their deals with the police and customs officials.

"We too had our dealings with the police and security forces. The Chief of Security Services would come to the office once a week to pick up his 'pourboire' (tip) for the weekend. Another man from Internal Affairs would also turn up on a Friday for his envelope. I forget how much I was advised to place in these envelopes but it would have been between US$500 and US$1,000. It was essential to maintain good relations with the police and security forces.

"Business here was a different story to Tshikapa. Initially we were told to buy up to a million, make a shipment, and we would get a speedy result. We did just that in the first week, but we didn't tell them that we had already bought another million. It didn't matter, and our results were always satisfactory. We were able to pay with a mixture of cash and 'Au porteur' dollar cheques, drawn on a Swiss bank account. These were the days before people worried about money laundering. The cheques had no name (no addressee), so if they were lost then it was the ultimate 'finders keepers'[17].

"When you're working with such large amounts, you get to a point where you're out of your comfort zone. By this, I mean pushing above the price that you valued. But the good thing about buying in volume was that unless you are very off base with your valuations, something bought too high is saved by a cheap parcel or stone.

"The bungalow was supposedly secure. It was an ordinary building with a gate and fence, but there was a steel door between the garage and the terrace at the back. There were metal gates at the front door of the house, and there was a waiting room, and the clients came in and presented the diamonds through a window (the same system as in Zaire), so there was a protective screen between us and them.

"With the larger parcels, it might take me one to two days to put a value on them and maybe a week to negotiate the price. Around 1980, I had a large parcel worth about three quarters of a million dollars. I worked at it all week, including negotiations with the client. It was Saturday lunchtime and I had weighed up the whole parcel and put it back into its original plastic bag, ready to return it to him. The client had kept pushing and pushing, and I had to be prepared to hand it back. The snag is that with any negotiation unless you say no thanks and good luck, it doesn't work. If you propose another dollar a carat or his expenses to complete the deal, he hasn't yet agreed to anything and meanwhile you are going to be paying more than you want to pay.

"I stopped negotiating and went back inside the house. The client was African Lebanese, Mohammed Guisee, and there was always something sour about him, always difficult. I came back outside with my bathing shorts on, a cold box and water ski under my arm. He looked aghast and exclaimed 'What are you doing? You can't leave now!' I replied 'Yes, I can. I'm going to ski on the river. You can take three quarters of a million dollars now or you can take back your diamonds. Bon weekend. I'm locking up.' Guisee took the deal. Then I had to write out several cheques for different amounts for him, because each cheque was money which he would then give to different people. Naturally all these cheques would roll back to France with the name Andrew Ward written on them.

"On one occasion, Glatt rang up and informed me "I've had the President of Credit Lyonnais on the phone. He's asking if your signature is good for a million." I said yes. Glatt never said goodbye at the end of a call. Clearly that would have been a waste of time and money.

"There were coaxers in Brazzaville as there had been in Tshikapa. I was lucky to know and work with the most wonderful man, Amadu Semmiga. He was tall, and his white boubou hid a painfully thin body. He had a wonderful sense of humour, and I can honestly say that he worked for the good of the office and for my reputation. He would cajole me to push harder to buy.

"If a client asked a very high price and refused to come down, I might burn it. This was a system that screwed the client and stopped anyone else buying it. I would ask 'Would you accept a price below $200,000?' This way, the client heard the amount but hadn't actually been offered it. When he left the office to go to the competition, he was confident he would get at least $200,000 as he believed I had offered that. When the competition turned him down on a figure above $200,000, he would come back to me. At that point, I'd remind him of the deal I'd offered of a figure below $200,000.

"Racism isn't reserved for whites only. Amadu had a poor view of the Congolese. He'd say in exasperation 'They're black,' which they were, being from the Equator. When I pointed out that he was far from white, he would respond that he was red. Coming from the desert, he was tall, and more brown than black in skin tone."

The company discouraged any socialising with their competitors, but Andy ignored this:

"Charlie Wisebaum was my favourite competitor. He worked alone, and his manner, humour, and psychology were Woody Allen par excellence. Charlie had a kosher kitchen and practiced the Jewish faith to the letter. For example, he would invite us out to dinner on a Friday evening, and then regret that he could not pay due to religious observance. Orthodox Jews are not permitted to use any gadget or electrical item on a Saturday, so to get our own back we would call him repeatedly, knowing he would be unable to answer. It would drive him crazy, and he'd mutter 'Those bastards, they know I can't answer the phone!'

"Charlie would often get buyer's remorse after he had purchased large stones, and he'd ring me up and say 'That's it, I've fucked up, I've paid too much.' I'd always say 'Send your man over with the stones.' Now at this point, I had two choices: tell Charlie the truth, that they were worth the money or say something like 'How much did you pay? That was very brave, Charlie.' As tempting as it was, I never took the second option.

"Despite all his strict religious standards of food hygiene, Charlie was fond of black flesh. Sometimes these girls would get too enthusiastic and keep coming around to his house, and he would become agitated, muttering 'They're not getting my cock!' We would say 'Don't give it to them, Charlie!'

"We would invite him over for BBQs. The old grill had had all sorts of meat cooked on it over the years, including pork, but we made a Herculean effort to clean it on his behalf. On those nights, he would have us go outside and spot three stars before he could have a first cigarette. And he could dance with a bottle of brandy on his head - he never dropped one. He was good and generous company.

"Our other competitor was Eli Arslainian who bought more than Charlie, but less than us. He would invite us home for dinner. He had a nice house and the most enormous dog. Tiberius was an Alsatian that had been owned by an Italian who had kept him chained up. The choice was that Eli took the dog or it would be destroyed. This dog changed completely once he had the run of the compound. Like security guards, he knew who was allowed into the house and who was not. God help anyone who came over the wall at night.

"An Armenian boy who worked with Eli was murdered during a robbery. Obviously the offices were open targets - everyone knew where they were and what we had in either diamonds or cash. The only thing I remember about this boy was that he lost his virginity on our sofa. He was very young. It was a futile end.

"We talked the company into letting us buy a new boat, a 19-foot SeaRay. I can remember we paid $25,000 for it. At the time, it was a lot of money, still we were making oodles of profit and it was deemed a good, healthy, outdoor activity.

"We all monoskied. The mighty Congo River provided miles of broad, flat waters. The idea of course is to turn abruptly, cutting the wave of the boat. For a brief moment you can be airborne, going faster than the boat itself. Steve would really stand the ski on its edge and turn, but I was also quite good on one ski. If you were really clever, you could be skiing along almost horizontal to the water.

"Clive had brought his own water ski and ski gloves from London. We used to tease him unmercifully as he would ski monotonously behind the boat forever. We would ski behind these large dugout canoes with Africans aboard, wave, and then turn sharply, soaking them. Then we'd make Clive go by afterwards, and even though he had no intention of soaking them they would, to our amusement, try to hit him with their oars. After Kinshasa, there are the Gats, huge rapids and enormous rocks for hundreds of miles, so if you went down there you'd be smashed to pieces before you got to the sea.

"One evening we brought a woman of the night back for Clive, who was a little prim. We said we'd pay her $100 to initiate Clive. We booted his door open and she went in, obviously pretty determined to earn her money. She chased him around the bedroom, and we could hear Clive protesting 'Oh no, madam, no thank you!' In the end, we paid her the money anyhow.

"Once when we dropped off Clive at the airport, we handed him the keys to open the boot and take his luggage. He set off through the airport, but suddenly realised he still had the house and car keys with him. So he came back, and called out to us 'I say, guys, I've still got the keys!' and he lobbed them over the barrier. If it had been us, we'd have kept the keys!

"Malaria was a constant occupational hazard. Despite taking the prescribed medication, I have had it three or four times. You feel hot and sweaty, and backache is another symptom, but the real clincher is when you're in bed and you feel cold to the point of shivering. Ironically, I have had it more often in the US and the UK. I was unfortunate enough to get hepatitis during a Brazzaville tour. That attacks your liver. The symptoms are fatigue, a temperature, yellow eyes, dark urine, and vomiting. The liver is unable to function properly, and even thinking about steak or fatty foods almost made me sick.

"Amadu called a doctor, who gave me an injection and a long list of medications, which included syringes. He also took me to the Congolese National Lab for a blood test. I remember seeing a child having blood taken from his neck. They sat me down in a large wooden chair and then stuck a needle in me that had been used before. It had been boiled, I imagine, and came from a test tube with cotton wool stuck in the top. HIV/AIDS had not been discovered at that time. Ignorance is bliss.

"They gave me a small waxed box, which we thought was for a urine sample. Our cook took delight, as did the rest of the staff, imagining the patron crapping into a small waxed box! There comes a moment in all our lives when we are emotionally or physically down, and don't know whether to laugh or cry. My moment, the final indignity was when we had no toilet paper and I had to wipe my arse on the Daily Telegraph!

"Amadu took great delight in taking me to the doctor's office every day. The waiting room was always full of people, but, regardless, we swept past them and saw the doctor without waiting. The doctor would give me a shot in the arse, but he would gently slap me several times first, so you never knew when he'd given you the injection. Amadu always left the office beaming.

"Harry and Maurice Mabongo were our guards. They were both either pigmies or simply quite short. They had a metal spear, which we took delight in throwing into the palm tree and watching them swinging on the end, trying to remove it. Harry always wore a flat hat, and someone gave him a watch, which he used to poke with his finger accusingly when asked the time.

"I met my first wife in Brazzaville. Patricia was working for a US NGO, Care, from Washington DC. The project was twofold if I remember. Inoculations and trying to re-educate local people to plant corn. Their traditional root plant manioc (aka fufu/cassava) is their staple diet. Boiled, this root vegetable has no real nutritional value, but is a cheap belly filler made more palatable with fish or meat sauce, and Africans across the continent have been eating it since the beginning of time. Cassava is white, and has the texture of a heavy dumpling. It tastes to me like wallpaper paste. Needless to say, the whole programme was doomed from the start.

"Patricia came to live with Steve and me. She left Care and got a job working for the US Embassy. This was good as she was paid in dollars, and after some negotiation the working hours suited her. Life was good, we were in love, and I was making money in a job I really enjoyed.

"I remember we had to get a new visa for her. The old visa expired when she left Care. Amado didn't enjoy going to the State Police, but he went all the same, and we got a ridiculous letter from the US Embassy requesting assistance. The letter was covered in wax seals and ribbon to give it more weight. Mission accomplished.

"Another incident stays in my memory: the night I spent in a Congolese jail. It all happened after we had been to dinner with some German Embassy friends. We were on the way home in two cars. We drove down a dark tree-lined street, and the driver ahead suddenly threw the jeep to the left, which gave me just enough time to shout 'what the ...?' as I ploughed into two police escort BMW bikes, parked with no lights and at an angle without reflectors.

"The cops appeared out of the darkness and they weren't pleased. I left Patricia locked in the car, and was managing to convince the police that I wasn't drunk just as our friends turned up, but didn't see the storm drain and put the right front tyre into it. At that point the police were convinced that both of us drivers were drunk. I got my friend out of the drain, and he reversed out of harm's way with instructions to fetch Amadu. I was given a choice at the station, to either go into the slammer or remain on a bench in the corridor... no choice, I can assure you. All the police on duty fell asleep, and I could easily have broken out of jail - tempting, but not a wise choice.

"In the morning, we were let out to use a tap in the courtyard to 'freshen up'. The guys from the slammer were mainly Zairois, semi-naked and they had been whipped with electrical flex. Amadu mercifully turned up with cash and with a number of clients happy to help.

It turned out that Amadu had been told what had happened the previous night but said "Leave him there, it'll do him good.

"Amadu really worked for the office. He knew the values of the stones too, and he would talk me up and talk down the client. He was tall and old, so he had respect. You could touch his boubou and keep pushing. Once when he was ill, he refused to go to hospital saying 'No, no, I would die there.'

"Amadou would come and ask for $50,000 cash from time to time. I'd take it out of the safe and give it to him. His son was going to Hong Kong to do business and he said I'd have the money back on Monday. He always repaid the money. The company didn't know anything about it or they would have had a fit. But I knew I could trust him. Every time we'd done a good tour, we'd put aside money for Amadou. It was ridiculous really because we were giving him far more than we were earning."

I asked Andy to explain why they rewarded Amadou so generously. His explanation was that Amadou was bringing in good business for the company and not doing anything dodgy for the client under the table. Their salaries were something else. Maybe there was also a sense of deferred gratification in the sense that if Andy did well by the company, he would move up in his career and earn more later.

The other thing that struck me on hearing Andy's stories was the risk of extreme danger experienced by him and his colleagues as well as their competitors such as the young Armenian boy. Thinking back to my own years of living in Mozambique during the civil war, I think you can become immune to the dangers of being attacked or killed especially when you are young. But then I never had a target on my back as the diamond traders did. I tried to understand why he was willing to put up with such a dangerous lifestyle.

"Once a week, we would drive the eight miles or so to the airport. The aircraft – Air France or Sabena – would be ready to depart. The airport perimeter had no fence, so we'd just drive straight onto the airfield and hand a box of diamonds with paperwork directly up into the open cargo hatch of the plane. That done, we'd set off back to the office. The first time I was in charge, I was told to go into the airport and 'dash' (tip) the manager. I returned, confident I'd achieved that task, but it turned out that I'd tipped the cleaner, who was always very happy to see me after that.

"When I look back now, I think how dangerous it all was. Everyone knew about our shipments, from the Mines Ministry (which would have had to come around to do the paperwork), to the airline company we shipped through, and possibly the Central Bank and the police. We could so easily have been ambushed, shot, and killed. A plainclothes armed policeman accompanied us when we shipped diamonds back to the UK and when we received dollars from Belgium, but he was paid virtually nothing and I've no doubt he would have shot us if he could have earned more from an armed gang or individual.

"One evening, having successfully made a shipment, we all had a few drinks on the terrace. Before taking his leave, the policeman decided to have one more for the road. He poured a neat vodka, enough to down an elephant, and knocked it back in one. The effect was almost immediate, like watching a cartoon. I took the staggering copper out to the street and hailed a taxi. The driver wasn't happy about his condition, but when I said he was State Police his attitude improved grudgingly. Before taking his leave, the policeman pulled out his semi-automatic pistol to give to me. Thinking I'd rather not take possession of the gun, I removed the bullets and handed it back to him. Some days later a very battered policeman turned up to reclaim his bullets. He had got out of the taxi and fallen down a deep concrete storm drain."

Andy was also sent to Bujumbura, the capital of Burundi, which was the other conduit for diamonds smuggled out of Zaire. Despite being a poor country, it exported ivory, gold and diamonds, turning a blind eye to all smuggling out of Zaire. The diamonds came from the Kivu region that borders Zambia. The mine, called Miba, produced thousands of carats, but mainly of industrial quality.

Andy described how the smuggling was carried out:

"Diamonds were stolen from the mine and packaged in fire hoses. These hoses were then woven in and around the chassis of Land Rovers and driven the thousand kilometres to Bujumbura on roads which were largely mud tracks crossing rivers through jungle. These guys knew how to deal with borders and police checkpoints.

"The Land Rovers were driven into our garage and the necessary dismantling of the vehicle took place. Thousands of carats were then weighed up from small plastic dustbins. But it was at this time that Zaire decided not to renew the contract with the Diamond Trading Company. As a punishment, the price of boart (the lowest quality diamond, one up from coal) was reduced from $2.5 to $1 a carat. This reduction in price greatly reduced the average price of industrial diamonds exported or smuggled from Zaire, and in effect it killed the business in Burundi."

Once again, his 'exhausting' days were spent by the hotel pool. Their driver would come to get them if any clients turned up at the gate. They also spent time on the lake. Burundi is a small mountainous country, one of four to border Lake Tanganyika which is the longest freshwater lake in the world. It is also the richest freshwater ecosystem in the world with about 2,000 species of fish, plants, crustaceans and birds, about 500 of which are not found anywhere else in the world.

At night they sometimes went fishing in a small trawler. The trawler would tow out six or eight small boats with lights on the back, and drop each off in turn 50 or 60 yards apart. They then waited for a couple of hours for the fish to rise, attracted by the lights. The captain would call to each boat, and the boats that had lured the most fish rowed slowly towards each other. The fish followed. The trawler dropped its net, encircling the boats and the fish. The net was closed, and strong arms pulled it over the trawler's side. Any fish the crew tried to hide were thrown over the side. It was amusing to see some of the fishermen with something still alive flapping about in their trousers.

At the weekends, they would take their powerboat out on the lake. The boat was large but slow, drank petrol, and was difficult to get fixed. The mornings were calm, but in the afternoon the wind would come up, making the lake quite choppy.

As the smuggled trade with Zaire came to an end, Andy and his colleague Mike were recalled to Brazzaville. For political reasons - given the satellite buying stations in Burundi and Brazzaville essentially bought diamonds stolen from the Miba mine - rather than fly via Kinshasa, they took the safer route flying from Bujumbura to Nairobi. He recounted:

"We had made Clive our replacement to sign for the diamond stock and the cash left in the handover, and to cover our travelling expenses for the next few days, we 'robbed', him so that we could enjoy ourselves. Cashed up, we set off for the best hotel in Nairobi, but on arrival we discovered that it was the Organisation of African Unity Week. We were lucky to find a cheap hotel, where the reception thought we were gay for sharing a room and a bed. We flew on to Johannesburg where we did stay at a good hotel, went out on a small safari, did some shopping, and eventually took the flight back to Brazzaville.

Without warning and due to downsizing, I was made redundant as a buyer. I was heartbroken because I loved the job, the freedom, excitement, responsibility, and challenge. Looking back, it was probably the best part of my working life, over all too quickly."

A stint back in London was followed by a posting to South Africa. By then, he had married Patricia and she accompanied him. He said:

"Readjusting to work in South Africa was hard. There were small-minded people with their own way of doing things - a far cry from the multimillion-dollar buying operation that I had managed. There was a 1950's type mentality. The De Beers Club which hosted events and all manner of sport had a gentlemen's bar. There were two full-sized snooker tables in a club-like atmosphere. Women were simply not allowed in. This sexist thinking was commonplace, but not easily tolerated by my American wife."

Back in London again, his old boss from Zaire days had been interviewing staff for a position in Bombay. The job entailed teaching valuation techniques to the Indian staff. Andy got the job and the two of them worked for a De Beers joint venture with the Indian government, called the Hindustan Diamond Company. Then he returned to London but carried on working with the Indian clients:

"After two years in Bombay, I was given the job of allocating all diamonds to Indian clients in India. I had my own office in 17 Charterhouse Street and a secretary. My job was to listen to the client brokers' pleas for a greater allocation of diamonds. It must be the only business where the client asks for more product and you, the seller, refuse.

"The job meant that I had to spend at least one week in the market every month. I was sometimes accompanied by a broker who wanted me to meet a client and be shown around his polishing factories. De Beers had a policy of allocating diamonds that reflected the clients' ability to manufacture. The reason for this was they didn't want diamond speculation as a result of oversupplying the market. In theory, the bigger the polishing capacity, the more diamonds would be supplied.

"Although I stayed at the Taj Mahal Hotel with generous expenses, those weeks were very tiring. Too much spicy food, too many late nights and early morning starts, too much alcohol amid high humidity. It was great during

European winters, but murder in the monsoon season May to September. This life wasn't as much fun as buying - it was more serious, there was more accountability, and ever greater scrutiny.

"This was the beginning of the end of our marriage. My wife was left on her own too often with our two sons to raise, and I missed too many birthdays and anniversaries. It was a theme that would follow us throughout, which couldn't have been helped as I was ambitious and didn't ever want to be part of the humdrum life at work in London.

"This too came to an abrupt end as company politics played its part. Not any reflection of my abilities, but it was a career of Snakes and Ladders, and I had had more than my fair share of ladders. In November 1987, after 15 years, I resigned and we moved to America - my wife, two children, and our border collie, and with no job prospects other than working in my in-laws' furniture factory.

"How the mighty had fallen. I was now living and working with my in-laws. There is something rather sobering about working on a shop floor with a staple gun having previously worked in suits, had a secretary, and flown business class to work on another continent. It was a huge change. I spent three years trawling Michigan for clients to buy the furniture we made, and it was soul-destroying - so many hillbillies trying to stick it to the sales guy.

"However, fate reached out. Pan Am was going out of business and offering cheap fares to London. My wife to her credit insisted that I go to London taking my oldest son with me to see my parents. There I met a friend who alerted me to a job with Diamond Counsellor International (DCI), Martyn Marriott's company. With recommendations and introductions from friends, I was back in London for a six-week interview. This included negotiations in London and Angola plus a month in Sierra Leone on my own valuing goods for the Sierra Leone government."

The dreary job of the furniture salesman had come to an end.

Chapter 7: The dupes of darling Rwanda

More than anywhere else, this tiny country in Central Africa elicited massive international outpourings of sympathy and aid after the genocide in 1994, though in recent years a more revisionist, questioning approach has been taken towards the so-called saviours of the country post-genocide in the form of President Paul Kagame and his Rwandan Patriotic Front Party.

Much has been written about the genocide and the society that Rwanda has become since then; films have been made, and controversy has gradually mushroomed over the role of Kagame and the tight security state that is present-day Rwanda, all fuelled by the British government's controversial 2022 policy proposal to use Rwanda as a processing point for refugees seeking sanctuary in the UK, which was subsequently reversed.

I was quite apprehensive about going to Rwanda for the first time in 2000, six years after the genocide. In 1994, the Rwandan government had adopted a policy in which everyone in the majority Hutu ethnic group was called upon to murder everyone in the Tutsi minority. This was not a new policy, and earlier rounds of killings and expulsions had begun with the Hutu revolution in 1959. The massacres in 1994 however were carried out with chilling speed, and about 800,000 people were killed in a hundred days using the low-cost, low-technology, commonly available tool used for working the land, the machete.

The United Nations decided for the first time in its existence to use the word genocide to describe this most efficient mass killing since the atomic bombs were dropped on Hiroshima and Nagasaki in World War II, and the rate of killing was equivalent to nearly three times the rate of Jews killed during the Holocaust.

No foreigner who visited Rwanda in the years after the genocide could remain unaffected by the horrific incidents of 1994. The country felt remarkably raw with grief to me in 2000. There was a government policy that every foreigner had to be shown some of the sites where the genocide had taken place, and I was taken to several churches where hundreds of skulls and bones were still piled up inside.

On one occasion, I was driven past a massive complex of buildings belonging to the Roman Catholic Church, which had played its own horrific role in allowing people to be butchered in its churches. I recall feeling intense anger towards the churches for yet another shocking example of how they had used their extensive power to abuse the individuals whose souls they are meant to save. I had just read a book by Philip Gourevitch called 'We Wish to Inform You That Tomorrow We Will be Killed With Our Families', a haunting sentence from one of the stories he told in the immediate aftermath of the genocide. Many accounts involved Catholic priests and

Seventh-Day Adventist pastors.[18] In a country where people always went to the Church with their problems, it was easy to encourage terrified people to gather at their churches and missions. Once in those so-called safe havens, they were massacred.

My task was to travel around the country to talk with communities, and identify the main barriers to education for a DFID project. This was my first introduction to an issue which has dogged so many education policies in Africa and possibly in developed countries, namely how to promote good technical education that results in jobs for young people. At that time, one was still able to use the terms Hutu and Tutsi, and I was clearly visiting plenty of communities and educational establishments in which most if not all of the youth were Hutus.

I was reminded only recently of the naked hatred I saw in their eyes when a former DFID Governance Advisor and colleague, Bill, used exactly the same words in describing his visit to rural areas in 2004. For some reason, I also recall above all else being shown around a technical college at which toilet paper was being made. I suppose what struck me most was that this must be a relatively simply product to make, and yet as I was invited to pull the paper off one roll, I discovered that it was patchy, insubstantial, and tore easily.

I stayed at the Hotel Mille Collines, which was where a most remarkable individual, hotelier Paul Rusesabagina, had worked tirelessly to save the lives of his family and over a thousand Rwandan refugees in 1994, a story akin to that of Schindler's, and which was made into the docudrama 'Hotel Rwanda' in 2004.

As the name of the hotel suggests, Rwanda is a country of a thousand hills, all beautifully terraced, superbly organised into tidy areas for plantations, with some mountains rising up to 4,500 metres in the north-west. Despite being relatively near the Equator, Rwanda's generally high altitude makes it a temperate, tropical highland, perfect for growing fruit, vegetables and flowers, especially roses, for export. Its clay soil supplies the many brickworks, and most buildings I came across were made with these red bricks, so that the country looked rather different to many others I had visited.

I was driven all over this small country, and struck by how well ordered everything appeared to be. There was no speeding, drivers obeyed the rules of the road, and this was the first time I had come across a courteous signalling code from truck drivers: as one approached, a left indicator signalled it was safe to overtake, while a right indicator meant overtaking was unsafe.

Like many aid workers who came to Rwanda in those days, I had the strong feeling that "we" must help the country to return to a semblance of normality and heal the wounds of the recent past. It was unusual to talk to anyone, from ministry colleagues to taxi drivers, who had not lost most or indeed all of their relatives during the genocide. And it seemed obvious in the early days that Rwandans were keen to make the most of international aid. The statistics appeared to show that aid projects had great results - although these results were later questioned - and the country was apparently improving in terms of many key social and economic indicators.

The orderliness, the pleasant hotels and wonderful choice of restaurants with high quality yet inexpensive food were obvious attractions. Rwanda is a coffee producer, and over the years coffee bars with all the elegant style and comfort of modern European cafés, libraries, and lounges had sprung up in the capital where one could enjoy 'the signature coffees of Rwanda' from the Kizi Rift Valley Region with their 'pecan, berry, and floral notes'. On later visits, I used to frequent a restaurant called Heaven, which was not a name used lightly. It was also a restaurant with a mission, namely to hire staff who were disabled. In recent years, it has apparently become a luxury boutique hotel and spa, visited by the likes of King Charles II and Queen Camilla in 2022.

I was not alone in feeling drawn to the country, and that it was worthwhile to work there because the senior leadership was determined to improve it, and corruption appeared not to be tolerated - a breath of fresh air to anyone a little jaded after working in so many countries where corruption was rife.

I did hear rumours that not all was as glossy as portrayed, and yet I put them to one side: what country is perfect, and after all they had suffered Rwanda deserved to be cut some slack. At the time of my first visit, I was also working in Angola, and would regularly attend British-Angola Forum meetings in Chatham House in London. De Beers would give an annual address to the Forum on what they were doing to address blood diamonds. At one meeting, the De Beers representative stated that Rwandan troops were looting the diamonds from mines in the DRC, and if anyone knew what was happening in those mines, they did. After the meeting, the young DFID Economic Advisor muttered to me "That was embarrassing", given DFID's whole-hearted endorsement of President Kagame.

On my second assignment in the late 2000s, Bill told me a story about Paul Kagame's regime. He was overseeing a project in the Ministry of Finance, led by a Cameroonian who was very upright and correct. The Cameroonian admitted to Bill that he had been asked by the Minister to help open off-shore accounts in France, Belgium and Switzerland. Since this was not a project activity, Bill asked if he was doing overtime 'off project'? The Cameroonian colleague clammed up, but Bill eventually dragged the information out of him.

It turned out these funds were not 'off budget', because they were never in the budget. The money was obtained from the sale of coltan from the Democratic Republic of the Congo, which arrived in Rwanda from across the border in Kivu once a week, and went to bank accounts directly linked to Kagame's family. This was in 2004, and when Bill reported it to DFID the British High Commission told him to keep it to himself. When he later asked Clare Short what had happened regarding his findings, she told him to fuck off, and that everyone knew Kagame was trying to track down Hutu killers and no more questions should be asked.

However, when a CNN story broke about Rwandan soldiers in Kivu camps looking for Hutus as well as minerals, Kagame denied it. At the time, DFID was paying 30 per cent of Rwanda's budget. It was the biggest per capita aid programme anywhere.

Clare Short told Bill "I've spoken to Paul", and Bill advised her to threaten to withdraw British funds. She did, and Kagame then admitted the truth about the troops, but said they were there for valid reasons of national security and protection.

The looting of minerals in the Democratic Republic of the Congo by Kagame proceeds unfettered today. In 2024, the BBC reported that Rubaya, the heart of coltan mining in the DRC, had been seized by the rebel group M23. This happened the same day that French President Macron called on neighbouring Rwanda to 'halt its support' for M23, which President Kagame denied giving. The DRC President, Tschisekedi, claimed the rebels were a front for what he called the 'expansionist aims' of Rwanda.[19]

As early as the year of the genocide itself, there were some inklings that Kagame's Rwanda Patriotic Front (RPF) party was not as honest as it purported to be. The United Nations Office of the High Commissioner for Refugees (UNHCR) had begun to receive reports of mass killings by the RPF in May 1994, but the influential human rights organisation African Rights dismissed any suggestion of massacres. The UN hired an experienced human rights researcher, Robert Gersony, who was shocked to discover up to 30,000 revenge killings inflicted by the RPF, but his findings were so embarrassing and politically inconvenient that they were pushed into the long grass.[20]

A French journalist I know, Bernard Debord, who visited Rwanda with a delegation of Amnesty International in 1994 and 1995 in the aftermath of the genocide, had similar reason to doubt that the RPF were as innocent as they appeared to be. He made two documentary films, one clandestinely inside the prison in Kigali. He had bribed the head of the prison with a TV antenna and some children's games to gain entry. Inside he found conditions which reminded him of images from Nazi concentration camps, with about 10,000 prisoners were huddled into a building designed to hold 600. No French media channel would air the documentary because France was too embarrassed to appear critical of Kagame's regime.

Bernard knew the former director of the Rwandan human rights organisation, Droits de l'homme,

Alphonse-Marie Nkubito, who was made Minister of Justice in July 1994 but later became critical of Kagame. Shortly after he was invited to Paris by Amnesty International he was found dead, presumed to have been poisoned. Also critical of Kagame was André Sibohana, a Hutu Roman Catholic priest and journalist, who had saved many Tutsis and won a prize with Reporters Without Frontiers.

Anglophone journalists and heads of foreign international agencies were charmed by Kagame and his closest advisors. According to Bill, the British, French, Germans, and the US all knew Kagame was behind the genocide. But without him in place, what would happen? There was no succession. Even now, 60 per cent of the budget is financed by foreign donors, and Kagame still criticises them, often in his own language, Kinyarwanda. And the more invested they become in this country, the more it becomes essential to justify all the aid.

Not only was there no institutional memory within the aid community pre-1994, but there was also a nationality and language barrier with the old guard being primarily French and French-speaking. It appeared to the new anglophone aid workers after 1994 that English was sufficient to communicate in Rwanda, but this only reinforced their limited contact with senior figures in the RPF who had predominantly but not exclusively been living pre-1994 as refugees in neighbouring English-speaking countries. I was one of the few people on the various projects who spoke fluent French, which meant that I could also communicate with the mainly Hutu community.

For most of the years when I worked on DFID funded programmes, it was clearly understood that one should coordinate and liaise with "like-minded donors", which chiefly meant the European Union, the Scandinavian countries, Canada, and sometimes the US. France was definitely not in this group, so we never spoke to French aid workers who might have told us a different story. On my second assignment in Rwanda in 2007, the last French person on the Adam Smith International project team left shortly after I arrived. He certainly embodied the old guard in many respects, not least because the new government had decided to embrace British public administration policies and practices, so the old legalist French administration was gradually being dropped.

In the ministries and agencies where I worked, most of the senior people spoke English, though there was usually one who was a French speaker and probably (not that one could say so) a Hutu. In the early days, we were expected to travel around the country to consult with local communities, and having French was certainly an opportunity to speak to more people although we were always accompanied by someone spying on any conversations with another staff member from the ministry or even a driver.

Next door to one ministry where I later worked, there was an organisation with the unwieldy title in three languages 'Commission to investigate the role of the French in the genocide'. I learnt only recently that shortly after the launch of this independent commission set up by the Rwandan government in 2006, French Human Rights judge Jean-Louis Bruguière accused the Rwandan President of shooting down the plane that sparked the genocide.[21]

The 2008 Commission report found France's role damning, so French diplomats were kicked out of the country[22], and from one day to the next French was banned as an official language. Although this should have made my life easier, it did not. I would attend meetings at which hardly anyone apart from the foreigners and senior staff spoke English, and although I used simple language and spoke slowly, there was non-comprehension in the eyes of most participants. I asked a Rwandan colleague how communication between Rwandans and foreigners would be possible in English, and she smirked: "On triche, nous sommes habitués." (We cheat, we are used to it).

This reminded me of one of Philip Gourevitch's anecdotes upon meeting a senior ranking Hutu in 1995 who told him that Rwandans can never be trusted, saying "Foreigners cannot know this place. We cheat. We repeat the same little things to you over and over and tell you nothing. Even among ourselves we lie. We have a habit of secrecy and suspicion. You can stay a whole year and you will not know what Rwandans think and what they are doing."[23]

Sadly, many of the worst practices of the Anciens Régimes are adopted by the new guard. Just as in Mozambique, where the government kept the pink building notoriously used as a torture camp by the Portuguese for the same purpose for its own enemies, so the RPF in Rwanda carried on a system used by the previous Hutu single party rule of 'one in ten', an informal system of policing that operated at village level, with one person reporting back on each cluster of ten houses across the whole country. After the genocide, files in the domestic intelligence service revealed that Rwanda was one of the most intensely monitored societies on earth, including 24-hour surveillance reports, records of intercepted telephone calls, and listening devices in hotels and embassies.[24]

One rather amusing but chilling example of the Rwandan Big Brother involved my colleague Bill. Having not worked in Africa for ten years, he had just come back to Rwanda for the first time. One Friday evening, dressed casually, he wandered over from his apartment to the nearby garage mini-shop, and an African kid stopped him to beg for money. Bill told me:

"I suddenly felt incensed about being regarded as a cash cow after all these years of aid and support flowing into the country, so I pointed to a nearby smartly dressed Rwandan about to climb into his expensive SUV and said to the kid 'Go and ask that man, he's rich.'"

One Monday morning I was sitting with about 20 ministry staff before a meeting. Unusually, they were chatting animatedly, and although they were conversing in the Kinyarwandan language, the occasional English word floated into the conversation. I was intrigued, and asked my neighbour what they were talking about. She told me "A white man refused to give a street child any money; he told him to ask a rich Rwandan man for money. We are saying that clearly this white man was only white on the outside, he was black on the inside."

According to Bernard Debord, white Europeans are regarded in Francophone Africa as 'les arbres à sous' (money trees). I have often pondered over the Rwandans apparent admiration for and amusement over the white man who was black on the inside. It struck me that they actually despise white foreigners for giving them money. They appear to approve of the uncharitable behaviour which they believe characterises Rwandans. Has aid contorted and twisted the mentality of Rwandans so much that they feel they have no responsibility to help each other, or is help only given to extended family and friends?

In 2009 I travelled around the country with a communications specialist, who among other accolades had been an advisor to President Reagan in the 1980s. Steve Massey had been brought into our project to produce communications materials for Citizen's Charters, which had been an innovation in the UK about 15 years earlier during John Major's premiership. The idea of the charters was to improve public services by making them more accountable, transparent in terms of costs and time frames, establishing a code of conduct and better value for money, and providing a clear means of redressing grievances. Rwanda seemed to buy into the idea, and our project was tasked with gathering all the necessary information to include in the charters.

However, due to time lapses in the contractual process, Steve arrived too early to be able to contribute to the project. We hadn't yet drafted the charters for which he was meant to produce communications messages to inform citizens. One might ask why his trip was not delayed. A brilliant cartoonist, he came and hung around our office, listening to our discussions and doodling on any scrap of paper to hand, launching into spontaneous scribbles until a mischievous and politically damning cartoon flew off the page within minutes.

Steve and I visited a few towns to ask administrators and local people about their expectations regarding public services. He suggested that in addition to our scheduled route and meetings, we should just stop at the roadside whenever we saw a few people and have a chat. He was quick to notice that no sooner had I started asking a few questions in French someone a little more smartly dressed would arrive on a bicycle, and surreptitiously insert himself into the group.

Steve's ensuing cartoon of these meetings was riotous. Someone presents "ordinary folk for you to interview" to me: a diplomat, a minister and an army general. One asks "You're English? My people summer in Poole ..." In another, I am sitting at a table with a plant on it across from an ordinary-looking citizen. I say "Feel free to say anything you want." The man points to the table: "Okay, the plant is bugged." Squeezed onto the same piece of paper, Steve drew a group of the famous mountain gorillas in a tree canopy[25], below which a park ranger explains their presence to a group of foreigners "They stay in the jungle because the silverback can't sign the paperwork permitting them to change villages."

The cartoons were a little incendiary, enough possibly to cause us some embarrassment if seen by Rwandan officials. Steve dedicated two of his doodles to me and, delighted and flattered though I was, I couldn't help feeling a little apprehensive about taking them with me out of the country. In the end, I inserted them between the pages of my work book. The second cartoon was a witty depiction of me carrying a suitcase home filled with ripe avocadoes. The cartoon, titled "After Hogarth: The Avocado Smuggler", shows the reaction of customs officers when my avocados prompt an alert on Kigali airport's x-ray machine. Two officers point a gun at me, another aims a nozzle from a box filled with "chemical weapons spray", while a fourth approaches me in heavily clad protective armour. Behind one official is a poster titled "Terrorist Fruit", depicting Osama Bin Laden holding an avocado.

Did it trouble us, the aid practitioners, that Rwanda was to all intents and purposes a police state, and that most likely any (and maybe there were actually many) dissenting voices were being squashed, suppressed and/or locked up? At that time, I didn't know about the political assassinations. Over the years, we continued to shrug it off, considering that the reported significant gains in development "results" (better schooling, health, and agriculture) made our efforts worthwhile and if the price was restricted individual freedoms, so be it.

In fact, it seemed to me at the time that there was an emerging dichotomy of countries where weak development and corruption went hand in hand with greater rights of free speech, while better development went along with restricted liberties. Rwanda's incredible statistics made it easy to overlook its predatory actions in countries such as the Democratic Republic of Congo, Uganda and Burundi.

Certainly, an authoritarian regime can at least make some good decisions fast. From one day to the next, Kagame banned all plastic bags on the grounds that, dumped on the ground as they frequently were, they formed ideal breeding grounds for malaria-ridden mosquitoes. Once when I arrived and walked into our office in the ministry carrying a duty-free bag of chocolates, my colleagues' first reaction, rather than the customary greeting, was to gape aghast at my bag. "What on earth's the matter?" I asked. The ban had been immediate and comprehensive. I think it even excluded the use of the infamous bags for carrying liquids on board aircraft in hand baggage. I had to congratulate the Rwandans for this fast action, considering years of consultations had left most European countries dithering, undecided between bans and imposing a small cost on plastic bags.

Maybe for many Rwandans the limits to their freedoms were a price worth paying, and we should not be ethnocentric by imposing our own values about liberal democracy? But on the other hand, were we less caring about these restrictions because we had lower standards for Africans whereas we are more outraged when such things occur in Europe, Bosnia and Russia?

From 2007, I started working on several core public administration reform projects in Rwanda. Following a relatively quiet period of work - I was contacted by Adam Smith International, which had won a contract in Rwanda. In their view, my relative lack of experience was compensated for by my French and one previous assignment in Rwanda. However, I was quite anxious about embarking on a new area of work.

Andy often said to me "I'm not well qualified like you. I was always winging it. It was good luck that things usually worked out fine, but there were times when I wondered if my valuations were very far off the others' valuations, which would have shown I was wrong."

"Well, just because I have a PhD and a few languages, don't think I wasn't winging it too. I'd often arrive in a new country with a company I'd never worked with before. Everyone expects you to be competent and capable, which is not that easy." These short, one-off, intensive assignments were a challenging and traditionally masculine way of operating. You were meant to arrive, get up to speed, zero in on the essential meetings and information gathering, and somehow come to rounded findings and conclusions on the last day while you were still drowning under a mountain of information and half-baked analysis. There was no scope to be intuitive, to reflect on anything beyond the end of your nose, think outside the box, or consider whether or not you should gather information from anywhere other than the usual sources.

An experienced DFID Advisor told me that women don't tend to work as consultants for more than about three years, though whether it is due to the masculine way of operating, the fact that most colleagues are older men often deeply entrenched in their formulaic approach to the job, or pressures on family life arising from the irregular and frequent travel that most women opt to work inside an organisation where conditions may be more stable. However, it suited me on the whole, though unlike many male consultants I tended to under rather than overcommit.

Apart from a small number of longer-term assignments with regular travel, my experience was typically feast or famine. After showing interest in an assignment, the dates for winning (or more often than not losing) the tender and the start dates for commencing work were invariably delayed for anything between one to six months. I wasn't willing to commit myself to back-to-back assignments or working on several projects simultaneously in a country where I would already be working nine to ten hours a day on a specific project.

Between 2007 and 2009, I carried out many assignments under the broad public administration reform programme in the Ministry for Public Service (MIFOTRA). The first one was the most challenging though. Having just won the programme, the young Project Director, Felix, was keen to prove our worth so he agreed to take on a previously unsuccessful job on the proviso that the local consultants whom we chose were approved by the Ministry of Local Government. He had an inkling that part of the problem in the previous assignment was that the ministry's agenda had been to employ Rwandans rather than Kenyans whom they already knew, and who would do their (possibly covert) bidding.

We were to carry out a so-called 'capacity building needs assessment' of all 30 district authorities with just 40 per cent of the original budget and in half the time. Given this short time frame, we opted to hire 30 consultants to cover one district each simultaneously. I worked with a brilliant Rwandan woman, Chantal, on the programme to come up with a checklist of all the material they would have to cover and how they should gather the information, and then trained all 30.

All the consultants were male, and 28 were francophone with just two English speakers, although all insisted (as I later discovered everyone did) that they were bilingual. I quickly learnt that this was not true, so I wrote training slides in English but spoke to them in French. They used to drive to the training sessions in their own smart cars, but would demand a car and all equipment in addition to a daily allowance for meals and any overnight stays.

Felix brought in a very able Kenyan woman, Irene, to organise the logistics. It was no mean feat to hire a fleet of 30 4x4 vehicles for a couple of weeks, but Irene did, and dealt with the 30 consultants moaning and bitching about not receiving higher daily allowances. Fortunately, Irene stuck to her guns and Felix stuck by Irene's judgement.

I was at times privy to these conversations, and it struck me that the Rwandans were quite rude and racist towards Irene, whom they referred to as 'the Luo'[26], which seemed decidedly two-faced given Rwanda had banned the official use of Hutu and Tutsi ethnic identification. I sometimes wonder whether such politically correct bans are aimed purely at white, liberal Europeans who will happily comply and won't ask questions about what is really happening under the surface.

On a later occasion, I met a DFID Advisor in Ethiopia who was Rwandan. Introductions over, my Ethiopian colleague immediately asked him if he was Hutu or Tutsi. The Rwandan was reproving, quoting the official line, but I looked on aghast as my Ethiopian colleague smirked and insisted on knowing the answer to the question. He knew why it mattered even if I didn't.

After we had successfully completed this assignment, I was asked to lead a small team to review 32 of the government's semi-autonomous agencies. Also known as QUANGOs, and in existence since the 19th century in the UK, these agencies have proliferated over the years and nowadays they employ the vast majority of UK civil servants and perform a range of functions such as the delivery of government services, provision of independent advice and expertise, and regulation of business. It is sometimes questionable whether they fulfil their intended purposes very effectively apart from absorbing or deflecting blame for bad performance[27], but a cynic might wonder if governments consider this in itself is not a rather useful role.

Tony Blair's very young team from his Africa Governance Initiative were in Rwanda and we were asked to liaise with them. One member was a young Asian woman, who eventually had to admit that she didn't know what a semi-autonomous agency was, which must be akin to a football fan not knowing about the World Cup.

As with any assignment in Rwanda, it was urgent that it was carried out lickety-split. I think we did an efficient job of quickly gathering information from these agencies' legal mandate, their staff and structure, and several of their 'customers'. For me, this was an interesting assignment, learning about the ins and outs of a multitude of very different organisations. In addition to managing the job, I carried out reviews of a few agencies myself. I was very impressed by the ombudsman, as were apparently many Rwandan citizens queueing outside the building with whom I was 'permitted' to talk.

I also reviewed the National Electoral Commission, which claimed that it needed more funding for educating the public about elections. I remember looking the Commissioner in the eye and saying to him with false innocence that given nearly 100 per cent of the population voted, they all seemed fairly aware about elections, and he should perhaps run a consultancy in Europe to advise how to educate that electorate. He couldn't keep a slightly wry look off his face, but he certainly wasn't going to tell me that what he considered problematic was the very fact that everyone voted for President Kagame.

Once we'd written up all 32 reports, we did a series of presentations to the government. Virtually no one attended apart from mid-ranking staff in those agencies. After one of the presentations, a highly experienced Governance Advisor whom we had brought in for the most sensitive agencies was spitting bullets of frustration at the company and DFID. It was a complete waste of time to do these reviews in the clear absence of political buy-in, and yet the following week I heard that the American Aid Agency, USAID, were meeting our ministry to propose carrying out reviews of agencies. It was an immediate, highly wasteful duplication of effort and resources.

In the early days of working on that programme, we used to stay at the Hotel Umubano, one of the older hotels in Kigali. Located close to our ministry, it was convenient and comfortable without being in any way luxurious, and the benefit for me was a pool and gym. I'd noticed over the years that consultants tend to fall into one of two camps: after work they either relax by drinking strong liquor or they rush off to use the sports facilities, and I veered towards the latter camp.

At weekends, plenty of Rwandan families would get together around the poolside and BBQ, which created a convivial atmosphere. There was a wonderful view of Rwanda's many hills beyond the pool, and skittish crested cranes stalked around the lawns looking haughty. In 2022, the hotel was bought up with a view to re-branding it as a smart, exclusive Mövenpick, but long before then my company had decided they could save some money by putting all its consultants in a rented house or apartment. Although I was not fond of spending weeks at a time in a hotel, the apartments tended to be quite soulless and restricted the opportunity to eat out and use sports facilities.

In those days, everyone who was anyone spent time in Rwanda. Arising early one morning at the Hotel Umubano to set off on a trip outside the capital, I found myself alone with Bob Geldof, who looked rather the worse for wear. Once while waiting at the gate to board my plane from Kigali, I nearly trod on a tiny woman crouched half-asleep under a blanket on the floor. When someone later helped her to her feet, I learnt it was Mia Farrow the actress, who was also a Goodwill Ambassador for UNICEF.

Biking across Africa, actors and bike fanatics Ewan McGregor and Charley Boorman, received an invitation to meet President Kagame in Kigali. The story I heard was that, conscious of having no smart clothing, they went shopping. In most African countries, shops selling European clothing and shoes tended to date back to about 1960 or possibly to the colonial era. It seemed that wealthy Africans bought their clothes overseas while the poor picked through charity cast-offs sold at markets. Apparently McGregor and Boorman turned up at the President's residence decked out in shirts with flashy patterns and long collars along with pointed crocodile shoes, only to be greeted by their host in jeans and a casual shirt.

My last assignment in Rwanda was in 2018. It put the nail in the coffin of my scepticism towards independent evaluation.

Chapter 8: Diamond poacher turned gamekeeper – the story of Martyn Marriott

A rather incredible and decidedly pro-African change in the diamond business began to take shape in the early 1970s, and it was partly down to one man who to this day remains largely unknown and unacknowledged. The change started in Botswana, a small country in Southern Africa which had been a British protectorate for 80 years, shortly after it became independent in 1965.

This man, Martyn Marriott, had the integrity to realise a change was due and he was able contribute his knowledge of the details and complexities of the diamond industry as a whole. He identified a suitable expert for the job of diamond valuer. As the only constant expatriate advisory member of the Botswana Government's negotiating team with De Beers for 13 years, he had the determination and not least the personal connections, to persuade, cajole, and muster the various conflicting interests to bring about a transformation.

Writers on Africa rarely mention that diamonds were the making of at least one country's economy. Sadly, just as journalists rarely report on the good news stories in Africa, there is a tendency to highlight the latest wars and elections which are invariably fought and contested. In the tiny hotel where I used to stay in Angola, I would often come across journalists who had come to write the latest news on the civil war. When I urged them to come to visit my project, which was having a positive impact on the lives of many of the poorest people in Luanda, they would demur: they had to focus on the war.

One writer explored how Angola moved from being a Stalinist to a capitalist state based on petroleum and diamonds.[28] Much evidence suggests that natural resource endowment is not positively correlated with economic development and social progress. It is rather the contrary: resource-rich countries are often corrupt and tend to be prone to conflict. All this is true but, as expert consultant Tony Hodges acknowledges, oil and diamonds were not the sole causes of Angola's many problems, and its mineral wealth did not cause the conflict. That began due to a nationalist revolt against an obdurate colonial power, and from Independence in 1975 it continued as a struggle between rival nationalist factions. However, the huge resources generated by oil, in particular in Angola, were a powerful motive to win or hold onto power.

Obviously the sale of natural resources also provides the means to purchase weapons, although wars have broken out in African countries with few or negligible natural resources. Rwanda must be one of the most egregious examples.

In her challenging book on the aid establishment[29], Dambisa Moyo cites Botswana as an African country which owes its economic success not to aid, but to strong institutions that have generated market-oriented incentives and protected investors' property rights, open competition, and a stable monetary policy and fiscal discipline. In 2002, Botswana had a GDP per capita of $8,170, which was more than four times the Sub-Saharan-African average. Crucially, Moyo states "By 2000 Botswana's aid share of national income stood at a mere 1.6 per cent, a shadow of the proportion it commands in much of Africa today. Botswana succeeded by ceasing to depend on aid."

This is true, but no mention is made of diamonds, which was a strange omission. The argument should be that sound institutions enable or foster natural resources being used for the good of the economy, as is the case with Norway's oil. To this day, Botswana's economy remains one of the largest in Africa at around $15,000 real GDP per capita, which is roughly three times that of Nigeria's and nearly four times the Sub-Saharan average. And its success still rests on its diamond industry.[30]

This is Martyn's extraordinary story in his own words:

"There were two phases in the story of the diamond business, pre- and post-Botswana. In the earlier phase, De Beers had a monopoly. This was the product of Sir Ernest and Harry Oppenheimer's attitude to the world, and basically most people in the diamond industry felt it was a good thing because it established a floor, and they built a stockpile so if the market was weak, they stockpiled goods. They also spent a huge amount on advertising, for instance they got involved in a huge advertising campaign in America over the engagement ring. That's where the engagement ring began: nearly everyone who gets engaged buys a diamond ring, and the same in Dubai, which is astonishing.

"This meant they were able to go to mining companies like Sierra Leone Selection Trust (SLST) and say we'll sell your diamonds and protect you from everything, and SLST bought into this deal originally as did everyone else, including the South African government, the Namibians and the Belgian Congo.

"The first hint of danger to that monopoly came at the beginning of my career. I joined the Diamond Trading Company, a De Beers company, in the late '50s. I had replied to an advertisement in The Economist seeking adventurous public schoolboys for exciting work overseas. At the time, the Diamond Trading Company was recruiting people to buy diamonds in West Africa, where extensive, uncontrolled diamond digging was disrupting the world diamond market."

Martyn's term 'uncontrolled diamond digging' referred to alluvial diamond digging. There is a crucial difference between the two main source of diamonds owing to their geographic formation and movement over the millennia. Diamonds are solid forms of carbon with their atoms arranged in crystal structures called diamond cubic. Most natural diamonds are between 1 billion and

3.5 billion years in age. Under high pressure and temperature, carbon-containing fluids dissolved various minerals and replaced them with diamonds. Many diamonds remain underground but hundreds to tens of million years ago, some were carried to the surface in volcanic eruptions and deposited in igneous rocks known as kimberlites and lamproites. The kimberlite rock is soft so it gets washed away and finds its way along rivers, typically getting parked in curves along the riverbeds. The diamonds found along 1,000s of miles of riverbeds – called 'alluvial' – cannot be cordoned off whereas the diamonds found underground can be mined in a controlled manner with fences and security.

The concern of De Beers was that the value of the diamonds they extracted from the mines could be undercut by the sale of alluvial stones by 100s of informal diamond diggers. Hence they wanted their buyers to 'mop up' alluvial diamonds as much as possible.

Martyn described his early years at De Beers.

"I learnt the basics of diamond sorting and valuation in addition to how the business was run from top to bottom. This included nine months in South Africa - six as a sorter in Kimberley and three at Ernest Oppenheimer and Sons in Johannesburg, the family company that effectively ran De Beers and Anglo American. I also had three months buying in Sierra Leone.

"I never became a diamond buyer as they decided I had the potential to be a future manager and trained me as such. On returning to London, I joined the sales department of the Diamond Trading Company as bag carrier for the executives who reorganised sales to Antwerp, and then was responsible for sales to Israel, including appointing the first DTC dealers there.

"At that time, the Oppenheimers had got together with the Russians, who were starting to produce diamonds. The Russians had exposed De Beers for being rather inefficient on the sales side. The diamond rush in West Africa had exposed the fact that De Beers' assortment and pricing mechanisms were out of kilter with the market, and this made it difficult to compete against experienced traders operating in Liberia. At the same time, it was clear that the rather relaxed deals that constituted their sales to a string of financiers needed reviewing.

"De Beers had already started improving their strategy, but they had a lot to do, and that's how I got involved, and then Andy because they had to send people to buy diamonds in places like Sierra Leone, the Ivory Coast, the Congo, and Guinea to tidy up their monopoly."

"'I'm intrigued to know what motivated you to support the diamond producers, that is the African governments?' I asked. I could have added that adventurous public schoolboys of the time were hardly closet supporters of Pan-African movements.

"The answer to this takes me back to 1963. I was asked to go out to Sierra Leone to manage the Diamond Corporation's business buying there. It was just after Independence, and my brief was to get to know the new government as much as anything else, and convince them of the continued benefit of its arrangements with De Beers. This was not difficult as the expatriate community in the country reflected Sierra Leone's importance in the world. I mean, Barclays didn't send their best people to Sierra Leone, nor did the smaller companies, so even the diplomats weren't the cream of the diplomatic corp. The Duke of Edinburgh once called Sierra Leone the arsehole of the Empire and it was known as the White Man's Grave!

"That was cruel because in fact Sierra Leone had the first university in Sub-Saharan Africa, Fourah Bay College[31], where many Nigerians and Ghanaians had studied, which meant that Sierra Leone had a huge influence over English-speaking Africa. When I got there, I found Sierra Leoneans were better educated and more amusing than the expatriates; they were charming and well educated. I had lots of African friends, and I was a sympathetic ear. They were great party people. There was a young gang of us, and we got on very well with the Sierra Leoneans. It was a lot of fun.

"It was my job to make sure the De Beers system was maintained. I believed in the principle of that system – I thought it was beneficial as a whole to preserve the monopoly and the way the industry was run, but it was quite a dirty business. There is no doubt that De Beers did take advantage of their situation, for instance buying diamonds from Namibia for perhaps 20 per cent less than they were worth. They had the expertise to value rough diamonds. Some people in the mining companies were beginning to acquire this skill. The producers were becoming suspicious of De Beers, and I wanted to smooth out their relationship with the producers.

"At that stage, I was trying to strengthen De Beers by making the situation more stable and less subject to abuse and malpractice, and I had some success, but after five years and having lived through three coups, my luck ran out and President Stevens decided to deport me. This was not surprising as I had been very good friends with the previous regime, to the extent of helping the Foreign Minister (to whose daughter I was godfather) seek asylum by taking him to the Guinea Embassy in the boot of my car.

"Back in London, there was nothing for me to do and I had obviously blotted my copybook, but I persuaded management to send me off on an executive development programme at the London Business School, which opened my eyes to quite a lot of things I wasn't aware of in management terms. On my return, I suggested that I might become corporate planner, only to be told 'Dear boy, the corporate plan is in Harry's head.' De Beers was run very much as a family business; one was knocking one's head against the family ceiling.

"So I decided to leave De Beers. There was no future there, and I thought I might go into politics - I was chairman of the local ward and had co-written a Bow Group pamphlet on international aid - or set myself up as a consultant to the diamond industry with two target markets: the diamond traders, whom I knew to be very badly run, and African governments. De Beers accepted this on a 'better the devil you know' basis, and helped me on my way.

"I thought I could advise people in the trade, and I also thought I could advise African producers on how they could maximise their profit, because although De Beers protected them, in practice they (De Beers) were busy screwing the Sierra Leone Selection Trust diamond mine in Sierra Leone, who were the first people to wake up to this. They got into bed with some major diamond businesses and tried to escape, but De Beers managed to keep them on board. I felt that there was scope for an association of African diamond producers to protect themselves.

"So I set out on a tour of the African diamond producers to promote the idea and sell my services. I visited Sierra Leone, Ghana, Angola, the Congo, South Africa, Namibia, and ended up in Botswana. Here is where the story really begins."

"Why were the other countries not interested?" I asked.

"Sierra Leone was vaguely interested. President Siaka Stevens asked me to write a report thinking I would do the dirty on De Beers, but I didn't, and I'm sure De Beers was looking after these African leaders in various ways. When I was based there, we bought a printing press for the party in power, and when they came to London they were put up in Park Lane rather than at a youth hostel. We felt that was appropriate. That was the line. A subtle way of corruption, which De Beers was extremely good at and I was good at it too. I had a huge expense account and put on wonderful parties. Half the cabinet ministers would come to them."

"So maybe some of the senior African government individuals were personally doing very nicely from De Beers even if their countries weren't, and they thought why 'rock the boat'?" I suggested.

"Yes, that sums it up nicely. Congo was total chaos. Ghana was interesting with President Nkrumah, but it went nowhere. However none of this did any harm as it demonstrated to the Africans that I was on their side.

"Botswana is where the story really begins, starting in the early 1970s. De Beers had discovered diamonds in Botswana on the eve of Independence. Its government was led by Sir Seretse Khama, tribal chief of the major tribe. He was well-educated and had qualified as a lawyer in the UK - overall a remarkable man. After being elected following Independence, he set about putting together a team to take over the running of the country from the rather elderly, second-rate British civil servants in place.

"The first thing was what to do about diamonds. Seretse Khama's team of bright young go-ahead Batswana, South Africans and British, set about negotiating a mining agreement with De Beers, advised by Professor Gordon Goundrey from Canada. I made contact with this group. And there was another group of British civil servants inherited from the Protectorate period, who were well meaning but thought it was wonderful that Botswana had discovered diamonds and that De Beers, a British company, was coming to do business there. Khama's young group said that's all very well, fine, but at a price!

"Professor Goundrey came up with the main contract, and I got involved in the marketing contract. It was clear that my knowledge and experience would be of use to the government, but first the opposition of the old civil service had to be overcome. Once this was done, funds had to be found to pay me, and an application for these to the UK Overseas Development Administration was made. This was initially strongly opposed by De Beers, but common sense prevailed and I was appointed Diamond Consultant.

"I persuaded the government it was correct to sell through De Beer's Central Selling Organisation (CSO), which had previously been known as The Syndicate. The Batswana just needed reassurance that they would be protected, that there would be stability, stockpiling, and advertising, and that it was worthwhile to pay De Beers' charge of 10 per cent for their marketing services. It was worth it, given the typical volatility of the market's highs and lows. So the Botswana government wanted this complicated agreement with De Beers.

"The key factor in the marketing agreement was how the diamonds would be valued. This was complex, as diamonds come in an enormous range of sizes, shapes, colours and qualities, and to value them you need a system of dividing them up into different categories and pricing these categories. You have a choice as to whether to put a parcel of diamonds into category A or B. When working for De Beers, you would always put it into Category B (a lower value category) so they would pay less tax and thereby make more money when selling. But there is always a margin between colours and shapes where a decision has to be made - either price x or x+1 or x-1.

"De Beers had developed a valuation system, but few people outside the group knew much about it. Various governments had employed independent diamond merchants to try and establish whether or not they were getting a fair price for their production, but I was aware that in practice De Beers could normally manipulate their system.

"De Beers proposed the Botswana diamonds be sorted by Diamond Development, which was a company in London that specialised in valuing. Basically Diamond

Development was just another De Beers front, but they had to start there so the first task was to persuade Diamond Development to up their game a bit, and the key to it all was having the diamonds properly valued, and the key to that was finding a government valuer who was committed and motivated.

"I had to find someone who was able to check the De Beers own valuation. I didn't know many of the De Beers diamond valuers, but fortunately I found the ideal man. Milos Viner had been the number two diamond man at the Diamond Trading Company in London, and its most successful buyer in West Africa. He had left the company because he realised how little De Beers actually knew about diamonds and how out of date their assortment was, and because he wanted to test his capabilities and theories by trading in the market. De Beers would not respond to his initiative of paying attention to so-called broken diamonds ('makeables'), which were really quite valuable.

"Milos made £70,000 (a lot of money in the early 1970s) in his first year of trading, albeit in a rising market. I persuaded him to let me put him forward as Valuer to the Botswana government, and Milos was marvellous. I had known him as a friend and I knew his capabilities. He had grit: he'd walked out of Czechoslovakia when the Russians moved in, and wanted to go to America to make his fortune. Milos was far and away the most successful diamond buyer Sierra Leone had ever had. By this time he was 40 or so, an idealist and quite arrogant. I said why not come to work for us? He saw the attraction of doing this. He wanted to take on De Beers and show them he could make quite sure Botswana got a good price.

"Milos and I formed a company, Diamond Counsellor International, to do the work and set about building a team to carry out the valuations. We had a five-year contract, which was renewed twice.

"We negotiated a 'master sample' for all the categories in terms of size, shape, and colour between De Beers and the government. This master sample was weighed and recorded, sealed and kept separate, and referred to if necessary in order to avoid any future disputes.

"However, I should also say that although my role was significant in terms of my knowledge of De Beers and bringing in Milos Viner, I was a small part of a team which played many other roles including the financial, legal and social aspects of the various negotiations.

"The original people around Sir Seretse were Quill Hermans, Permanent Secretary in Finance who went on to become Governor of the Bank of Botswana, Peter Landell-Mills, Director of Economic Affairs, who went on to a career with the International Bank for Reconstruction and Development, and John Syson in the Office of the President. Economic advice was contributed by Bob Dean, Charles Johnson, now a successful novelist, Steve Lewis, the distinguished US economist and others. Amongst the legal advisers was Peter Eigen, who went on to found Transparency International. Mining expertise was provided from Canada. I and all these people worked with and for a host of extremely competent and hard working Batswana civil servants and politicians - these were the people who bore the responsibility for approving and implementing anything we outsiders suggested. The presidential oversight from Sir Seretse Khama and later Quett Masire was a dominating force."

"What evidence is there that your involvement in Botswana resulted in an increase in revenue from diamonds over the period?" I asked.

"Firstly, revenue from diamonds increased predominantly due to an expansion in production. As Diamond Consultant, I also pointed out to the government that its agreement with De Beers effectively limited the production of the Orapa mine to a level below what its size and value merited. Fortunately, Professor Goundrey had included a clause in the original agreement that allowed renegotiation if anything proved wrong, so the government opened negotiations to increase production, which was eventually doubled.

"Although the first round of sorting of the Orapa production diamonds was carried out by Diamond Development, part of the De Beers/government agreement was that the work should be transferred to Botswana as soon as possible and Batswana trained to do it.

"De Beers then discovered an even bigger and richer mine at Jwaneng. The government put together a team of which I was a member to negotiate with De Beers. The basis of the financial arrangements sought by government was the recent UK arrangement for North Sea oil: a tax system that maximised its take based on the profitability of the project. The government also wanted greater control of the business as it was so dominant in the Botswana economy. Seretse Khama's young group of advisors saw that the diamond industry could absorb a higher tax rate than it had anywhere else before, and basically share in the profit of the mining business by becoming a shareholder.

"I proposed that the Botswana government should consider the idea of a joint 50/50 company with De Beers as was already in place in Tanzania in terms of the governance. Although the tax regime was under negotiation, it was already part of the deal that 50 per cent of the profits after tax would accrue to the government through the 50/50 company, and this was taken into account in the ensuing negotiation covering royalties, profits tax, etc., which resulted in the government getting 80 per cent of the gross income.

"Secondly, we hoped that from day one the diamonds would be valued properly - and we know this for a fact from our valuation of the very first shipment out of Botswana. It's a silly story, but in their own valuation of the industrial diamonds De Beers used the South African price book rather than the London price book, which meant the shipment would have been sold 20 per cent cheaper. When Milos and I pointed this out to them, the De Beers team reacted 'Oh Good Heavens, what an extraordinary thing! A pure administrative error, and how clever of you to notice! Yes of course you must have the London price.' De Beers also agreed to build a specialised sorting office in Gaborone to compensate the government for their error."

"Did De Beers challenge your valuations at any time?" I questioned Martyn.

"No, the top management of De Beers always took the line that 'we always buy at the right price and we are happy with the profits we make. We don't cheat you!' We employed some of the best people De Beers had had, so there was mutual respect. It was a competitive thing, and we knew the game was maximising vs minimising.

"Working for the Botswana government led to the identification of many areas, large and small, where there was potential for cultural conflict. De Beers mines operated in closed towns for security reasons, and the Batswana rightly did not like this. A director of Sierra Leone Selection Trust once commented to me that we were dragging De Beers into the 20th century! There were also problems over the supply of water to the mine. Eventually De Beers agreed to an open town at Jwaneng and opened up Orapa. With the aid of an Australian firm, they also found water for Jwaneng in the desert. The government asked me to come to Botswana and co-ordinate the De Beers/government involvement in the company, and brief the government board members on the running of the joint company.

"Botswana also had a pretty sensible monetary policy, because they had this huge revenue from diamonds, and they didn't have to do anything else. They are obsessed with cattle and would go to their cattle base for weekends. So that explains a basic difference between them and the Sierra Leoneans, who are totally dependent on diamonds. Botswana was also keen on developing manufacturing, although personally I think it was a mistake to try to build a factory for diamonds; they should have asked De Beers to build a car industry or something else in order to diversify the economy.

"Our contract in Botswana was not renewed in 1983. We were undercut by some members of our own tender team who put in a separate bid, and I suspect there was a degree of corruption. We never bribed anyone, but there were signs that corruption was beginning later in our time there. But that's another story.

"I have been approached by a PhD student from the LSE, who is writing a thesis on the relationship between De Beers and the Botswana government. He tells me that he was amused to come across some old minutes of a meeting at the Botswana Ministry of Finance, in which they were discussing my fees. The Minister of Finance took the position that I had contributed so greatly to the economy that whatever fee I asked for was worth it!

"The next big step occurred when I was asked by the Argyle Mine in Australia to introduce them to the complexities of the diamond world. I advised them to sell through the Central Selling Organisation, and this led to us being appointed their valuer. The Argyle production was low quality with a preponderance of brown diamonds, and as such particularly hard to fit into the De Beers systems. It also had the benefit of producing a few pink diamonds, which were exceptionally valuable.

"The Australians were full of new ideas about diamonds that were anathema to De Beers. They wanted De Beers to advertise brown diamonds more, and to pay very high prices for small pinks. The large quantities of low-quality diamonds were difficult for De Beers to sell, and there were personality clashes between the executives on both sides. Milos and I did our best to paper over the cracks, but eventually the Australians, by then owned by RTZ, decided to go their own way.

"This, combined with the discovery of diamonds in Canada, finally led to the end of the Sir Ernest and Harry Oppenheimer Central Selling Organisation selling system.

"I was also involved in Canada, being retained by the Government of the Northwest Territories to advise them on the diamond business. They accepted my advice to have a Government Valuer to check sales, but appointed a different diamond consulting company rather than DCI.

"Meanwhile Namibia became independent in 1990. Before this, as part of the preparation for Independence, I had trained some Namibian nationals for diamond industry participation for the United Nations. Also, Milos had a friend who was an arms dealer with a good relationship with SWAPO, so we were in a good position to bid for the government diamond valuer role there, which we got in 1994 and held till 2004, when we lost a tender. We had trained two good Namibians and, as suspected, they put in a lower bid against us. But in Namibia the process is reasonably transparent, and one can apply to look at bidding documents. Six months later we saw them, and discovered a mathematical miscalculation resulting in our tender coming out with fewer points. Although it is quite complicated to assess the tenders, this was clearly a mistake. So what to do? Go to law? We decided to leave it alone eventually. Our fixer was heavily involved in arms dealing in South Africa, and we sat down with him and his partner. They said 'We don't want to get into a fight with the Namibian government. We advise you it would be difficult for everyone.' I was quite keen to challenge as I'm that sort of person.

"During the lull after the Botswana contract I had contact with Angola, but that's another story. Then in 1985, I had a visit from an emissary of President Momoh in Sierra

Leone seeking my advice on what to do to reorganise the diamond trade there - official exports had fallen to tens of thousands of dollars. I duly visited and reported to him. A key element was to improve security, and I agreed to take on the role of Government Diamond Valuer on condition they employed a proper security firm to stop the smuggling. I arranged for a good British firm, but they gave the contract to someone else who was quite useless, however at the time smuggling was completely endemic to avoid paying the 10 per cent export duty.

"Subsequently, I was invited to advise the government of Guinea about organising its diamond exports, and as a result we became its Valuer too. This was followed by a successful bid for a similar role in Liberia."

"What was the story about blood diamonds?" I asked.

"At the turn of the century, there was a great fuss about blood diamonds: diamonds financing or fuelling the civil wars in Sierra Leone and Angola. The diamond production from these two countries amounted to between 4 and 15 per cent of world diamond production, but the blood diamond narrative was a compelling one.

"As a result of UN interest, and also interest from De Beers who were extremely concerned at the bad publicity, a conference was called in Kimberley in 2000. Prior to the conference, an association of major diamond companies and producers, the World Diamond Council, was established by the diamond trade to ensure its point of view was put forward.

"I attended the Kimberley conference as part of the Sierra Leone and Angola delegations and as a member of the World Diamond Council. The development of the certification scheme was done by the Belgians. The extraordinary thing was that of all the people at that conference, virtually none of them knew anything about diamonds! Only three people understood: me, the Director of Mines from Sierra Leone, and Martin Rapaport.

"Trying to explain to civil servants from all over the world the intricacies of the diamond business was quite a challenge. They thought diamonds were just like any other commodity. They had no idea of the complexity of the product (different sizes, shapes, colours, and qualities), nor of the difference between industrial mining and alluvial mining by diggers. It fell to me and Ousman Kamara, the Sierra Leone Mines Director, to educate them, an uphill struggle further complicated by Rapaport, who had a crackpot scheme of his own for Africa.

"The meeting and subsequent ones were also prolonged by two extraneous political issues: the Chinese/Taiwan political division, and the requirement by the EU delegate that he alone rather than individual members like the UK and Belgium should speak for the EU. The Belgians and the UK wanted their own involvement and knew about diamonds, whereas the EU delegate didn't. But as soon as anyone from the UK or Belgium got up to speak, the EU delegate said they were out of order. He was a terrible man, determined that everything had to go through him.

"At the end of the day, we are left with an enormous bureaucracy which meets twice a year but achieves very little because its decisions have to be consensual. The Kimberley Process has also become a bit of a jolly. If you are from Yugoslavia for instance, you've got nothing to contribute so you just enjoy it. The Kimberley Process really fulfilled its role ages ago, but you can't disband it.

"Out of it all eventually came the Kimberley Process Certificate, which all diamond imports and exports had to have. This successfully "closed the stable door long after the civil war horses had bolted", but has had some effect on minor incursions. It also had an enormous impact on the diamond trade as it made trading on the black market in order to avoid export duty very difficult. It could also be of some use meeting the burden of identification of small productions in the current sanctions against Russia. Although the G7 have decided they want to implement sanctions, the problem is how. All diamonds over one carat have to be certified. Blockchain is a chain of pieces of paper through to the source. It's chaotic, and no one knows how to create it."

After my discussion with Martyn, I pondered on whether there were any objective assessments of these efforts to reform the diamond industry which was kick-started as far back as the early 1970s in Botswana. I turned to one of De Beers' harshest and most knowledgeable critics, the NGO Global Witness, who were one of the first members of the Kimberley Process and prepared to believe in the early years that the certification process was working or – in the words of the one of the Global Witness directors I spoke to at the time – at least it gave sufficient legitimacy to attempts to stop blood diamonds that it was no longer worthwhile for Global Witness to keep campaigning on the issue.

Later, Global Witness dropped out of the Kimberley Process, because they felt it was toothless. They argued that the Kimberley Process's remit should be extended to cover diamonds coming from everywhere in the world where production was associated with human rights abuses, but by 2019 they had acknowledged grudgingly that the World Diamond Council was taking serious steps to put its house in order.

Referring to two statements issued by the World Diamond Council in which they recognised serious human rights concerns in the diamond sector, Global Witness wrote "These statements represent the diamond industry's strongest critique yet of the government-led certification scheme, the Kimberley Process (KP), in recognition of its failure to break links between diamonds and human rights abuses. Alongside this acknowledgement, the World Diamond Council highlights the critical need for industry itself to take steps towards responsible diamond sourcing ... It remains to be seen if these recent releases are empty words intended to burnish the sector's tarnished image or if they represent a genuine and welcome shift towards recognition that the diamond industry must embrace transparent and responsible business conduct."[32]

There has to be an overwhelming interest in the diamond industry to break any link with human rights abuses for various reasons. Customers are increasingly more concerned about ethically traded goods, though how far this is simply a voiced concern versus an actual change in their purchasing behaviour is something I am not sure about. But no one needs to buy diamond jewellery and they have no utility, so the allure and mystique of real diamonds unfettered by association with conflict are crucial to sales. As a veteran De Beers marketing executive often said "we are not in the business of selling diamonds, we are selling emotions." Bad publicity can be catastrophic.

A leading diamond trade journalist and industry analyst commissioned to investigate the possible links between diamonds and the financing of terrorism after 9/11 in 2001 found the industry had been quick to embrace new anti-money laundering and anti-terrorist financing. The De Beers Chairman, Nicky Oppenheimer stated "Let us make no mistake, there are new challenges ahead ... Foremost amongst those challenges is the vulnerability of the diamond and jewelry industry – as with other commodities – to misuse and abuse by criminals and the perpetrators of terror."[33]

The emotional appeal of diamonds becomes especially important when laboratory-produced gem-quality diamonds are on the increase. The lab-grown diamonds are cheaper, without flaws and without any ethical issues, apart from the impact on the environment of the enormous energy and heat required to produce them.

As for the industrial need for diamonds, there is a clear advantage in synthetic stones because they all come out as uniform crystals with so many microns. This means they wear out evenly, which is important for drilling and polishing applications. Laboratory-grown diamonds were first produced in the 1950s by General Electric, and later De Beers set up a factory in Shannon, Ireland, for manufacturing synthetic diamonds for commercial purposes such as drilling and polishing. But it was only more recently that manufacturers were able to produce larger and higher-quality gemstones.

Chapter 9: Nigeria – rats, bats and The Aid Show

I first went to Nigeria for two weeks in 1997 in a team comprising an official from the Department for International Development (DFID), a few doctors and me. We travelled all over the country to evaluate a health project under the aegis of the Bamako Health Initiative. Given the size of the country, two weeks was a short time but I did at least get a sense of the society and culture, and the geographically distinct areas.

Our team travelled in convoy with a few Land Rovers, one of which was designated as the gift vehicle due the large number and bulky size of the gifts we were given by local communities, none of which were we entitled to keep on the grounds that they might be regarded as bribes. However, I held onto a gourd, which had been lightly engraved and was apparently used as a wind instrument.

We stayed in some pretty run-down hotels and motels during our trip. My bed in one of these establishments had a sagging mattress and seemed quite dirty, so I decided to sleep on a sheet spread over a few sofa cushions placed on top of the thick brown shag pile carpet. In the morning from the bathroom I spotted a large rat moving along the floor and had a horrible vision of this creature crawling over me in the night.

Then I returned in 2015 to a very different type of aid project and a different way of working. The most obvious contrast was that I only ever went to Abuja, the capital, where I was ferried to and from the airport and between the project office, a few government departments, and my hotel. It was a bit like being inside 'The Truman Show', the 1998 American psychological comedy-drama directed by Peter Weir.

Where The Truman Show instilled messages about the dangers of travelling and the virtues of staying home to prevent the protagonist Truman Burbank from escaping the colossal soundstage, The Aid Show's message was about the ineffectiveness of travelling, because everything we needed to do and understand started and ended with the central (federal) government, in particular the Ministry of Finance. There was no point in leaving the capital to see how project money was spent or asking what citizens felt about public services. Arriving tired after the flight, I would occasionally wonder what would happen if the driver were to turn right rather than left onto the highway between the airport and Abuja. Would we hit the buffers, the edge of the film set?

In addition to geography, much else had changed in The Aid Show in the intervening years.
The first most obvious difference was that aid budgets had risen enormously, seven and a half-fold in the case of the UK, where in the 24 years between 1997 and 2020, they went from about £2.6 billion to about £14.5 billion.

The largest amount spent per geographical region went to Africa. In real terms, global aid spending in 2019 was over twice as high as in 2000, and nearly five times as high as in 1960.[34]

Taking a step back for a moment, up till the end of the Second World War aid had been as much about donor largesse as political control over colonies. After the War, the goals of aid were buying influence for the West versus the East during the Cold War. Interestingly, one could say that this goal has returned to become the blatant issue in 2025 during the new Trump Administration in America, where the key questions to aid beneficiaries are more likely to be "What have you done for us lately? Why should we help you?"

After the collapse of the Soviet Union in 1991, a supposedly moral dimension to aid was introduced as the aim became the reduction of poverty. When the new Labour government came to power in the UK in 1997, aid grew in importance and became a separate government department, the DFID. An aid commitment to give 0.7 per cent of wealthier nations' Gross National Income (GNI) dating back to 1970 was reinforced at various Aid Summits, and the UK achieved this target in 2013.

What was done with all this extra money though? Was it enough? Was it too much?

Advocates claim that aid does produce results, but the problem is that there is not enough, that a vast increase is needed to escape persistent poverty traps. The current reason why the situation is dire is due to slow post-Covid recovery. One writer wrote recently "Undeniably this money [aid] does good. Tens of millions would be at dire risk without it. But vast areas of need remain unmet. And it is hard to point to big success stories."[35]

Many writers say that aid is doing the wrong things, and if it were to do the right things, it would have a greater impact. Veteran writer William Easterly says that much fails because there is too much top-down, supply-side planning, and not enough searching for the nature of problems and what solutions might work.[36]

Others say that certain types of aid work better, for instance giving cash to the poorest makes more sense than funding health and education on the grounds that people themselves know how best to use their resources.

One particularly bold writer insists that not only has aid had no demonstrable impact on development – as demonstrated by numerous studies by the World Bank and others - but its effects are not even benign. It is actually malignant - it is the problem. Dambisa Moyo describes a vicious cycle in which aid fosters corruption, corrupt governments interfere with the rule of law and transparent institutions, making investment unattractive, which in turn reduces economic growth, which leads to fewer jobs and therefore more poverty. In response to growing poverty, donors give more aid, and this continues the downward spiral of poverty.[37]

From my own experience, it seems that the huge increase in the aid budget over these years had various generally negative consequences in terms of how aid was delivered and the results it produced.

While DFID's budget grew massively, there was no corresponding rise in staff numbers, which remained at around 1,900 between 2005 and 2015 when the aid budget was growing at its fastest pace[38]. This meant that civil servants needed quick, easy ways to get money out of the door with low transaction costs – the time they spent on administering the transfer of funds - so that they could still look productive and effective.

DFID staff adapted by phasing out small-sector projects. Large projects morphed into enormous programmes run by contractors composed of mega consortia, the members of which are natural competitors.

New ways of spending money involved passing it on to other institutions. More went to the so-called multilateral agencies,[39] which had absorbed 37 per cent of the budget by 2022, the highest percentage since 2014. My colleague Bill told me "We contributed to trust funds typically managed by the World Bank and when things went wrong, we blamed lax World Bank rules. However, the Public Accounts Committee got wind of this and said to DFID that regardless of who was managing the money, DFID had a fiduciary responsibility to exercise control over UK funds."

Another significant change was that the skilled experts among development staff and consultants were replaced by generalists. Going back to the 1960s, after independence had been declared in the ex-British colonies, there was a five-year transfer of power during which the British Overseas Development Administration (ODA) put in place the Overseas Supplement Advisory Scheme (OSAS) to provide technical expertise in education, health, geology and veterinary skills to the new governments. Many OSAS officers were Indian and East African.

From about 1990, the Overseas Development Administration (ODA) gradually began to replace them with Technical Cooperation Officers who were accomplished in their fields of expertise. When the ODA became the Department for International Development (DFID), they started to employ companies to run projects, initially with a full-time DFID staff member embedded in the project, who would play an active role and frequently be on teams of project reviews. However as time went on, DFID staff had less and less connection with the companies they contracted to run the projects, and technical expertise was in the hands of generalists.

According my former colleague, Mr P "In the 1990s, suitable consultants required only one qualification – proven experience in the form of a relevant career history. One was told that a good consultant should have no hair, with grey hair the absolute minimum requirement. This is in total contrast to the current situation, where overnight apparently a degree in international development transforms people into experts in health, education, transport, energy, global warming, etc."

With so much money swilling around and rather few experts, one of the easy options was to pour massive amounts of aid funding into capacity building. Capacity is a misnomer because it generally applies to units of measure. Elsewhere in the public and private sectors, skills and competence (and correspondingly incompetence) are the correct terms. Yet capacity building has endured the ravages of aid fashion. It seems to be a politically neutral term which is devoid of any suggestion of corruption or malfeasance, which makes it easier to propose to a developing country. Because it is a little difficult to measure – and whilst global indicators of economic and social development do not improve - the resort to yet more capacity building is commonplace.

Ironically, the diamond reformers reached an end point in building skills and competence early on. Martyn Marriott's company committed to training government officers to value diamonds and put in place systems and structures for operating a government valuation agency. Within a few years, some governments (Botswana, Namibia, Sierra Leone, and Guinea to all intents and purposes) no longer needed the international expert assistance, and the Marriotts had virtually done themselves out of a job. Why were the diamond experts so much more effective than the aid experts? It seems to me that the government diamond valuation officials had a clear interest and incentive in learning the skills: once acquired, these officials would be well paid through a percentage or merely the success of the diamond export sales. They were not dependent on foreign aid.

The political profile of aid was raised as budgets soared, and overtly or covertly the "c" word – corruption – was mentioned and efforts made to address it, but to little avail. My colleague from Rwanda, Bill, provided some background here: "Starting in the early '90s, DFID led on establishing Anti-Corruption Commissions. The first one was in Zambia. Kenya, Ghana, Botswana, Sierra Leone, etc. followed. I argued that setting up these commissions was an acknowledgment by DFID that the law enforcement and judiciary were failing as they would normally deal with corruption. I was ignored. The symptom was ignored. Big fish were never prosecuted, and in Kenya this was exposed by Edward Clay[40], who was persona non grata in the Foreign and Commonwealth Office as he did not play the game."

Mr P went on: "One contractor delivered an inception report, setting out the approach to a project. The approach included oversight measures to ensure project funds were not abused, but the client wouldn't accept it because they'd rather have no project than not be able to steal the money. So the inception report was not approved, and the consultant went to the donor who knew exactly what was happening but wouldn't intervene. The net result was that the project did not proceed and the contractor did not get paid for work already done. If the contractor caves in, as most do by rejigging the project so the clients can steal the money, the donor is happy.

"I was asked to write a manual for the Audit Office to stop corruption. This was ridiculous: by the time it got to audit, it would be too late, the money already gone and not coming back. So I asked 'What makes you think this piece of rubbish will do anything to stop corruption? No, I won't do it because a manual can't stop corruption.' They got someone else to produce the manual. It was shocking. All it did was describe auditing. You could get a book on that from Amazon. But the people writing these terms of reference don't know the subject. No one queries it - it ticks the box, and the budget is spent. But I can't do this, I couldn't justify it as a chartered accountant. I'd be kicked out of my profession. What makes you think I should shoot myself in the foot?"

Nigeria has frequently ranked as the largest recipient of UK aid in Africa, and even the second largest recipient in absolute terms[41], despite very high levels of corruption and despite its status as a middle-income economy, with a mixed economy and emerging market.[42]

One could say that this economy developed despite the predatory behaviour of the government, and it is probably to the credit of the assertive and inventive (or should I say argumentative and stroppy, which I intend as a compliment) nature of so many Nigerians that they have achieved so much.

A Nigerian colleague, Sam Unom, cited successes of local entrepreneurs and innovators who, long neglected by or flying under the radar of official enterprise promotion agencies, have created a manufacturing hub in the southeast town of Nnewi, forged an informal economy estimated at an uncounted 35 per cent of the official GDP, created a movie industry (Nollywood) that is the second largest in the world, and expanded the country's telecoms and finance sectors through innovations in consumerisation, among several other breakthroughs. According to Sam, all over Africa these self-driven and self-regulated entrepreneurs-on-the-margins are finding ways to generate value outside the purview of asphyxiating, irregular state institutions. And despite being a member of OPEC, Nigeria is in no way dependent upon the petroleum industry, which only accounts for around five to six per cent of GDP.

Not surprisingly, given the assertive Nigerian character, the question of the role of colonialism would emerge during discussions about economic development and corruption. Writing in the Harvard Africa Policy journal, Sam maintained "It's all good to look at initial starting conditions around 1960 and proceed to call out African countries for lagging behind their Asian peers. It is also perfectly fine to denounce the corruption and policy failures of these African stragglers. But it is important to remember that there was one crucial difference in the starting conditions. India and Indians already existed before colonialism came and went. In contrast, there was nothing like Nigeria or Nigerians and nothing like Cameroon or Cameroonians before colonialists decreed them into existence, and soon afterwards left a legacy of artificial countries with irregular institutions that had yet to be bedded or embedded."[43]

In fact, India and Indians did not exist before colonialism and the first Indian constitution used the names Bharat and India in acknowledgement of the historical and cultural significance of both terms.

One response to Sam's piece by another Nigerian, Tersoo, challenged the emphasis on their colonial legacy "Sam, I enjoyed reading your thoughts on the subject and they are quite revealing. However, my position always is the unique human ability to think and proffer workable solutions in the face of daunting challenges. Why should we find it difficult to resolve the question of irregular institutions several decades post-Independence? If institutions that were anchored to strong communist ideologies could be transformed to capitalist and more open ways of engagement, methinks we could not be boxed in by the foundational cracks of the colonial era after so many years."

A top Nigerian businessman and one of Africa's richest men, Tony Elumelu, made a similar point in an interview in 2024 when asked why Nigeria had failed to live up to its post-Independence potential. The interviewer argued that colonialism and imperialism had set Africa back. Tony conceded "They did, but those also affected India and other economies. Why do you keep crying over this and not taking this into our hands? ... We got independence in 1960 - 64 years [ago], please. We shouldn't still be talking about this. We should move on. It's arguable that the country they bequeathed to us was better than the country we have today."[44]

Between 2015 and 2018, I worked on two public administration projects in Nigeria, one of which could be considered relatively small, cohesive, and effective, while the other was huge and epitomised many of the worst consequences and aspects of the great increase in aid budget spending.

The first project had the title The Federal Public Administration Reform Programme (FEPAR), and a budget of £34 million over a five-year period. Run by the consulting company Atos, it had managed to bring together a number of experienced Nigerians with a few foreigners on short-term contracts. My Atos boss from the Ethiopia project had suggested that I come to work on this one to write up the results and lessons. The project had an interesting perspective: it recognised the influence of politics head on, and sought to act in a 'politically smart' way to address corruption.

At the time, some of the more critical aid practitioners were identifying a way of understanding why so many aid projects failed. This understanding lay in biology. In the 19th century, biologists observed a phenomenon they named isomorphic mimicry, the process by which one organism mimics another to gain an evolutionary advantage. One example is the cuckoo. Rather than raising their own babies, cuckoos use mimicry to pass the responsibility to another bird. They even imitate their target bird's biochemistry by disguising their eggs in the same colours and patterns as the host's.

Applied to aid, isomorphic mimicry happens when government bodies create the outward appearance of highly functioning development institutions in order to conceal their dysfunction. Isomorphic mimicry both produces and enables persistent failure. It is so pervasive because it is attractive to African government reformers and, paradoxically, development agencies themselves play a strong role in promoting and sustaining failure. They encourage developing country governments to adopt the right policies and organisation charts, and to pursue so-called best practice or world-class reforms, without actually creating or supporting the conditions in which real reform and progress take place.[45]

Bill said "As an insider with DFID, we were well aware of the influence of powerful elites, but naively thought that we could change things. You will see that in the public financial management area, the recipient countries played the development partners by repeating the same projects with different sponsors. This has been going on with projects in the same areas of public financial management for 30+ years with no noticeable improvement. Tanzania is on Phase V, with continuous external support over 20 years and the same issues being rolled over. Currently the European Commission is financing this."

When projects are proposed by donors, individual interests are prominent, with rather little concern about the long-term development goals. Bill told me "The first questions African countries ask are what happens to the project equipment (cars, computers, etc.) at the end of the project, and how many foreign study tours and training sessions will be provided. Training workshops are seen as an opportunity for a free lunch, and they provide an easy way for consultants to be seen to be doing something. The technical objectives of the project are tolerated to get the 'gifts'."

Mr P recounted "A local guy had been appointed because of his good reputation for not filling his pockets. He told me every time bigger projects are announced, Nigerian delegations start appearing. All these people turn up and say I know great people, they are the ideal people for your project. And one thing he's learnt is that every time a recommendation comes in that way, never touch a single one of them because they're all going to feed – they want to get their man in there for a slice of the action, to get their hands on the money."

Sam once asked me "Which country has the best financial and anti-corruption laws in the world?" You won't want to guess that the answer is Nigeria, but it is actually true. And yet Nigeria ranked 145th out of 180 countries on the international Corruption Perception Index in 2023. I would put my money on those anti-corruption laws having been written by IMF or World Bank-funded consultants, with only a passing nod from the government.

And yet Nigeria also had a few organisations which ran extremely efficiently and where there was zero tolerance for corruption. Nigerians refer to these agencies as "islands of excellence", and I was introduced to the head of one of them, the Federal Procurement Bureau. He described the measures he had put in place to prevent corruption in an organisation which frequently provides rich pickings for corrupt practices in many countries. The example which stuck in my mind was his induction training course for new recruits. On the last day of training, he would take the recruits to a prison to spend a whole day of full immersion as a prisoner. He smiled as he described to me how the recruits were obliged to wear prison uniform, eat the food and be locked up in their cells, the routine of every prisoner. At the end of the day, he would say to these young men and women "If I ever catch you cheating or stealing, this is where you will end up!"

Many of the Nigerians working on the FEPAR project had worked or were still working part-time on several other donor projects, including our sister project on public administration reform, which ran at state level. That state project did all the international best practice so-called "tried and tested" activities of putting new systems (human resources, IT, budgeting, etc.) in place, and ran training programmes. It was the perfect example of isomorphic mimicry: promoting and sustaining failure.

Since I was tasked with drawing out the lessons of the FEPAR project, I asked several of the Nigerians "Tell me honestly – and I have no vested interest here - which of these projects do you think has the greatest chance of doing some good and bringing about change?"

They all said the federal programme was best, and they were enthusiastic about its scope for undermining corruption and patronage. The state project paid their fees, but didn't challenge the state governments. One of them said "The state project doesn't deliver anything. It's just the same stuff all the time.'"

To my mind, the strange thing was that our funder DFID always seemed very critical of our federal project while the state project was the teacher's pet. Our project scored A twice and B once over three annual reviews, compared with six A+ in the state project.[46] I can now see that it was easier to judge success in the state project. For instance, so many training sessions completed, so many systems in place. If you are trying to act in a politically smart way, it is less obvious how you measure your success because you have to devote a lot of time to assessing the vested interests of many players, to test and see what has the greatest chance of working. And some of those tests will fail, only to be regarded as a project failure and a waste of time and budget.

A striking example of FEPAR's politically smart work was how they addressed suspected fraud and corruption in the oil sector. Despite being an OPEC oil producer, Nigeria had no refineries at the time.[47] It therefore had to import refined petroleum products and it chose to subsidise the imports, supposedly as a benefit to citizens. But with little verification, subsidy claims and payments made to oil marketers shot through the roof. Subsidy payments accounted for over 22 per cent of the total 2012 federal government-approved budget of ₦4,697 billion (approx. USD 13 billion in 2020).

The typical donor agency reaction would have been to tell the government that subsidies were a bad thing and should be dropped. The politically smart thing to do was to play along with the subsidy regime and seek to help the government to make it work better. FEPAR staff knew that the petroleum subsidy regime was founded on a deep-seated political patronage and rent-seeking system. Attempting an outright cancellation would have elicited a fight-back from some of the political elite.

Instead, by paying for consultants to be based in the Oil and Gas Division of the Federal Ministry of Finance to develop a petroleum subsidy tracking model to match subsidy claims with a database of petroleum product imports, our project team smartly evaded the political challenge. They first sought buy-in from the Ministry of

Finance prior to launching the initiative. The model helped reduce the government's petroleum subsidy payments from ₦1,050 billion in 2012 to ₦505 billion in 2013. The amount saved was greater than the total budget for the health sector that year.

I liked to hope that perhaps the oil subsidy tracking was a success which would last over time, but I suppose the risk was that after the project came to an end, the situation would return to business as usual, which it did according to my former colleague Sam. However, perhaps our project's success did somehow influence the new President, Bola Tinubu, to take action because on day one of his premiership in 2023, he took the radical step of removing this ruinously expensive fuel subsidy entirely. And other FEPAR initiatives apparently stood the test of time including our advice on how to close or merge duplicating parastatal organisations.

Whilst working on the FEPAR project, I would typically spend two to three weeks in Abuja at a time. Everyone on the project, foreign and Nigerian (who were largely based in Lagos, commuting weekly to Abuja), was put up at the Sheraton Hotel in Abuja, which was comfortable enough though not on a par with many of its flagship branches. In any case, it was a considerable step up from dirty brown shag pile carpeting inhabited by rats.

We all soon earned enough points to become card-carrying Executive Club members at the Sheraton, which brought us a range of privileges including the use of a special lounge with free breakfast.

"Aha, it's good to know that aid money is being well spent on you lot," commented Andy. The teasing and mocking ramped up over time. I discovered that I had an intolerance of gluten and dairy, which made it quite difficult to eat at restaurants. When I alerted the charming Executive Guest Manager to my dietary needs, he immediately arranged a meeting for me with the hotel's Executive Chef, who asked me to let him know everything I could not eat and everything I could and liked eating. Furthermore, he said he would send me a message each afternoon to ask what I would like to eat that day, at what time and at which of the hotel's restaurants, and he personally would supervise the cooking of my dinner. If he himself was not working that day, he would appoint another person to follow through with my dinner order.

Fortunately, a lot of West African food is naturally gluten and dairy free and excellent to boot. There were jollof rice (rice cooked in onion, garlic and tomato among other ingredients), various meats, a green vegetable like spinach finely chopped and cooked with dried fish for added flavour, and delicious fried plantain (a less sweet type of banana). The fresh tropical were delicious: papayas, mangos and bananas. There was also fufu, a staple in many West African countries, made from fermented cassava. However, it sticks to the upper palate of your mouth, a most unpleasant experience. I decided that you have to be born West African to appreciate fufu.

"You are being spoilt rotten, and all at the expense of the taxpayer! Your Executive Chef is providing you with six star hotel service," Andy would exclaim. He was probably right. I would write outstanding reviews of the Sheraton Abuja, which rather stood out from the rest of the less complimentary reviews. What did I care if some of the equipment in the rooms – lights, television, air conditioning – was faulty?

The Sheraton Abuja was situated in grounds with a modicum of wildlife. The garden was home to a bright yellow weaver oriole bird colony. I could watch these beautiful birds with fascination as they built, entered and exited their nests, which hung from a thread from the branches of the flame of the forest (also known as flamboyant) trees with their fiery orange-red flowers, a supremely clever way to prevent predators from entering. These trees are revered in Africa, and their flowers, bark, leaves and seed gum are used for medicinal purposes.

Other trees in the garden hosted a huge colony of bats. As light faded towards sunset, the bats would rouse themselves and start flying around, littering the skyline like errant warplanes. I later discovered that Nigeria holds a third of Africa's total bat diversity with at least a hundred species. This was hardly a wild game safari experience with the "big five", but it enlivened my stays at the Sheraton.

There was a good-sized outdoor swimming pool, and I seemed to be one of the few guests to make use of it ("Yes, yes, I know I am spoilt rotten."). However, one evening I arrived to discover lots of young boys and girls were having fun playing in the water. I was disappointed not to be able to swim laps that day, but to my surprise, the woman apparently supervising all the children immediately instructed them in a loud voice to move to one side of the pool to let me swim undisturbed.

Slightly intrigued by this very courteous and unexpected behaviour, I started talking to her, and thanked her for her consideration. She, Kathy, was an American who had lived in Nigeria for about 30 years and had set up a small orphanage taking in babies and young children, most of whom had been abandoned due to poverty, HIV, or other severe health conditions. She ran the orphanage on a shoestring. A few individuals donated funds or provided other assistance. One had persuaded the Sheraton manager to let her use the swimming pool, one of the few luxuries that she and the children could enjoy. Whenever there was some extra funding, she would run health clinics.

I saw a lot of Kathy and her kids over the three years I travelled to Nigeria, and observed how this remarkable woman supported so many happy and thriving children, though a few died young from severe health conditions. I suspect that regulations in America or Europe would have found fault with how the orphanage was run, but it was obvious to me and some of my colleagues who also got to know Kathy that she was greatly loved, and that the children thrived under her care.

Early on, she was offered funding by foreign donors, but later she turned them down, saying taking foreign money was more trouble than it was worth: "I always remember my friend saying to me when I accepted a USAID-funded grant 'You will get burned, but take the money. The HIV work is in their hands, so beware.' And burned I was, but I survived. It was not easy."

Essentially, Kathy preferred to operate without all the donor requirements such as accounting, reporting, focusing on the latest donor fad, etc., and in any case she was quite capable of achieving a lot with far less money than the average project:

"Take the UNICEF VIP latrine initiative. They were well planned, except the people with the idea did not realise construction was far beyond the available funds of most villagers, so a VIP latrine-paid project became a chief's showcase with the one or two latrines that were used by his family, the pastor's family, etc., and the open ground well continued to be contaminated when the rains started, and typhoid and cholera were rife.

"Our youth team in the bush dug three latrines at our centre using only one bag of cement to make three 'no fall in' platforms, then used whatever junk was available to make walls. We even had a bamboo vent, and soon requests were coming in for junk latrines. Now they are the norm in that district, but we didn't do much, just sent our expert trained villagers in on 'latrine building day', followed by a communal meal. In the end, with a grant of just £200 we helped build 54 wells with pumps, MANY latrines, and paid for the petrol to travel to the various locations. A friend subsidised the work with some cement. One lady even built a latrine with growing walls, and it looked so nice. Others copied hers, and criticised my ugly junk latrines!"

Kathy is still living in Nigeria, though in poorer health, and many years later the orphanage is now more or less run by some of the young people whom she originally took in as babies, while others have gone on to work and university without losing contact and still support the orphanage. These days, if I am asked which charity in Africa is worthwhile supporting, I think of Kathy first.

After the FEPAR project ended, DFID launched a new programme with a budget of £133 million, which combined three previously separate projects, and was called PERL (Partnership to Engage, Reform and Learn). This programme was massive, with a very large consortium of companies, all of whom were ordinarily competitors. It morphed into a new phase and was set to run for eight years when I last checked. Fifteen implementing organisations are named on the FCDO Development Tracker, but I know that this does not include further sub-contracting, because I was contracted through a company which is not listed. Most partners were private consulting companies, others were NGOs and academic or policy bodies.

Some individuals were openly hostile towards other companies. I was invited to sit in on one meeting where a man from the former state project was very aggressive towards me. He kept saying in loud asides to his neighbour "Why is she here? She shouldn't be at this meeting." When I was asked to provide some information from another part of the programme, he kept talking loudly to drown me out.

I chose to say nothing. I'm not sure if this was out of cowardice or delayed reaction to bullying - or if I was more concerned about what might happen if I lost my temper. I don't often get angry, but when I do the anger gets out of control. I should have turned to him and told him to shut the fuck up, instead of which I simply ignored him, raised my voice and carried on talking to the rest of the group. No one else in the meeting told him to be quiet. Afterwards I put in a complaint, which I suspect went nowhere although the programme management team obviously had to pay lip service.

This programme became entrenched in confusion, incompetence, and poor management as far as I could see. My part remained the federal section, managed by a new Nigerian manager, who had been recruited because he was a political activist. That was all very well, but he treated the programme as a cash cow to fund his other activities, and frequently did not come into the office for days at a time. None of the Nigerian colleagues complained. They all accepted this situation with occasional mirth or an ironic comment.

I was given an assignment on one visit, which I duly completed. My terms of reference for the next assignment were only given to me verbally upon my arrival, and were identical. When I pointed this out, it was fluffed over. Instead I was asked to attend some meetings and workshops organised by other colleagues. Not only was this a waste of my time and their budget, it was a thoroughly disheartening experience. At one workshop I attended, the participants were asked to make a note of their hopes and concerns. Their overriding concern was that the workshop would go over old ground and waste their time. By the end of the day, I could see that this concern had been played out.

On another occasion, I sat in on a meeting attended by a lot of people from different civil society organisations. It was not clear what the purpose was, the organiser did not ask anyone to take notes, and it seemed purely an exercise in box-ticking that so many organisations had been consulted, like the initial meetings with NGOs in the World Bank in Guinea all those years ago. Smart political work had apparently flown out of the window. Although I was asked to go back to Nigeria on this programme, I told them I was no longer available, but when I talked to the one Nigerian whom I esteemed was doing seriously good work, I was surprised that she was surprised about my decision. Perhaps it was just obvious to her that consultants keep on going until they are no longer invited.

"Why won't you go back?" Andy asked me. "I would just be going to earn a fee; I wouldn't be doing anything useful," I replied. Predictably, he countered "Why do you care? Take the money. Everyone else will." Fortunately, by then I had earned and saved enough to feel that I could indulge my conscience and not just take the money.

Chapter 10: Government diamond valuation in Sierra Leone

Just 10 years separated my last school holiday in Sierra Leone and Andy's first job with the Marriotts in 1991. The days of the Wild West were over and the aim of the work was to assist the government of Sierra Leone to improve its revenue from diamond exports.

I have heard Andy's stories about working in Sierra Leone often, and they become more elaborate and funnier with the retelling. Quite a few involve policemen and women in Freetown. He was once stopped for driving an "unsanitary" vehicle. In buoyant mood, he asked the traffic cop to accompany him to the station to point out where there was a penalty in the regulations for driving a dirty car. The charge was soon dropped, though not before the policeman asked for some money for his family.

On another occasion, while talking on his mobile phone with a colleague, Mustapha, he realised he had caught the eye of two policewomen who were about to pull him over. He came to a halt, while continuing to talk, saying "Mus, I can't tell you how lucky I am, I have just been stopped by the most beautiful policewomen in Sierra Leone."

"The women raised their eyebrows and chuckled. Thus charmed, they told me to move on without asking for a bribe."

I asked him to tell me more about his job and life in Sierra Leone.

"It was the wet season, June or July, when I first went to Sierra Leone. Martyn Marriott had taken me on a tour of the contracts he had won, so I started with some work in London, after which we went to Angola for a week or so and then onto Sierra Leone. In Freetown, Martyn introduced me to the Government Gold and Diamond Office (GGDO) whereupon he let me get on with it as it was less important than their Angolan work. There were fewer politics there than in Angola. My job as Government Diamond Valuer was to value the diamonds conservatively at reasonable market value for tax purposes.

"Before DCI won that contract, there had been no official exports, just smuggling. And it was not cost- or risk-free - you had to pay bribes along the way, and your diamonds could be confiscated if you were caught. Alternatively, the trusted courier might decide that this was his retirement, steal the lot and disappear.

"I went to Sierra Leone for a month on, month off for the first few years. I lived in two places - in the early days it was the Lakka Cotton Club, 13 miles outside town, a holiday resort for French tourists by the beach. The building was like a tea plantation house, open up top on all sides. It overlooked the pool and the sea, and the rooms were small bungalows. It was French-run, not a great hotel but better than the Hotel Mama Yoko, which was state-owned and poorly run.

"Pierre the manager and I became good friends, and I was well looked after. During the dry season, the place was full of tourists brought in by bus from the airport. In the wet season the hotel was closed, but Pierre and I camped down there regardless. We would go out into Freetown in the evenings.

"In the old days getting to town was not easy as the road was covered in water-filled potholes. It was a great shame that the tarmac road built by the British around the Peninsula had not been maintained and became a mud track. The road followed the illegally tapped water pipeline from Guma Dam built by Taylor Woodrow in the 1960s. As the population of Freetown expanded, there was increasingly haphazard housing development along the road. Houses were built on very steep slopes where trees had been removed, and sometimes mudslides would kill people.

"Later I moved to stay with my Lebanese friend Billy who was much closer to the office and centre of Freetown. The city of Freetown was plagued by twin problems of electricity and water - the infrastructure of the city was never designed for so many inhabitants. Fuel was supposed to be delivered in 50-litre barrels to the power station, but it would frequently be misappropriated. Fortunately, in more recent years a generator ship was brought in, and connected up to the power grid, thereby removing the possibility of stealing the oil.

"Billy had a large generator. His man would tap on his window when the power went off and on to ask Billy to switch to or from the generator. I didn't even have to get out of bed. He used to make tons of food, and we'd have nice meals and he'd send the rest out to the guards. The only way I could pay him back was to buy sushi up the road."

"What was the work like?" I asked.

"The day started at a leisurely pace, because people would make appointments from 10am and either turn up on time, late, or not at all. It was haphazard. I was always at the office by 9.30 in case there were any earlier clients, and to ensure I would find a parking spot. The office was in the Central Bank on Siaka Stevens Street, plumb in the middle of town and close to the famous Cotton Tree, symbol of freedom from slavery, and near the post office and American Embassy. Unfortunately, this iconic symbol which had stood there for over 400 years was blown over in a storm in 2023.

"State House was right across the road, where there were trees with giant bats that flew during daylight. The GGDO was initially on the 6th floor of the Central Bank, and this gave clients a sense of security when they brought their diamonds in: there were plenty of guards around. The head of the bank was very grand, and when he went out to lunch work ground to a halt.

"We had quite a lot of staff in the office. A peculiar thing about GGDO was that it was a parastatal which means the government let you get on with running the agency, but if you made any surplus money, as we did, it was paid to the Treasury. The Government Representative, the GGDO office manager, the accountant, secretaries and chaps helped me with the evaluations.

"As the General Manager of the GGDO, I came to realise there were various tensions and exploitative practices - angles were played for individual benefit. The accountant was difficult. When anyone went to him to apply for reimbursement, for medical expenses for example which covered their whole family, he would always expect a percentage. Mustapha told me about this, and I went straight to the accountant and told him to give them the money. Anyone there with a little power over someone else would use it.

"In the GGDO, there was a gold section as well, but all that happened there was that one of the men would do an acid test on any gold that was brought into the office. This didn't happen very often; gold was essentially smuggled out of Sierra Leone into Guinea. It was a form of currency for cross-border traders.

"Work was sporadic. Someone would come in with a stone or a parcel, and they would get the same treatment as anyone else, no matter what they brought in. The few mining companies in the country would make an appointment to cover all the paperwork and shipping. If there was no work, I went to lunch and would come back to the office, and then go home possibly without having done anything.

"A licence system was in place for possession, trading or exporting of diamonds. Licences to possess diamonds cost less than those for export. Licence fees differed, depending on whether licence holders were Sierra Leonean or expatriates. Some smaller dealers would have a licence to possess diamonds, but would export them for a fee through larger export licence holders."

"Did the Lebanese pay the same licence fee as Sierra Leoneans?" I asked.

"A good question. The trouble was the Lebanese didn't have the same rights as local Sierra Leoneans, even after they had lived in the country for two to three generations. They would gripe about it.

"Exporting diamonds was an arduous task. You came in for your valuation and an export stamp. Then you had to go to Customs downtown in Kissey, and it took forever to get the right papers, then onto the government building to get a signature from the Minister who might or might not be there. And woe betide you if you wanted to come in the morning and ship in the evening - while you went off to get the paperwork, we would hold onto the diamonds.

"Later we were able to convince the government of the benefits of one-stop shopping, so Customs came to us. With the Kimberley Process, they would then have to go to the Minister of Mines to get that certificate. But at least it was only one other stop.

"In the early days, they would pay us in cash in Leones for the export duty. The denominations were very small, so at times payment would be brought to the office in a trunk. Being scrupulously honest, Mustapha would count the Leones, until I'd tell him to stop counting as he would wear the notes out. You had to open the blocks of notes to check smaller notes were not mixed in with larger ones. Later it was done by bank transfer, so handling filthy cash came to an end. Once all these papers were in order, the diamonds would be wrapped up in a box, sealed with wax and lovely red ribbon, and then put into a plastic bag with a letter for Customs at Lunghi Airport. The box was sealed so securely that you couldn't add anything to it.

"The export duty was three per cent of the value of the diamonds, which was fairly standard throughout the region. Someone from USAID invited me to dinner, and they couldn't believe how little the government took in tax on diamond exports. They said they were going upcountry to learn about diamond mining, but it turned out it was just a one-day trip. So I thought, really, what will they learn in that time? They were only ticking boxes and it was a waste of time.

"And don't forget the government was in effect just selling licences to exporters, they weren't investing in anything at all. So if you don't take on any risk, why should you get anything back? They were not giving anything, they were not a shareholder."

Martyn Marriott added more background to my question: "As I'm sure you appreciate, Sierra Leone and Botswana are completely different. In Botswana the mines are kimberlite pipes, which can be fenced in. They are also remote and serviced by towns built for that purpose. In Sierra Leone the mining is mainly alluvial, spread over wide areas and, although Sierra Leone Selection Trust [the company my father had worked for] built a town at Yengema to service their mining, the town of Koidu is close by and a hive of illicit activity. Bear in mind also that Botswana was ruled by Seretse Khama, a true democrat, and Sierra Leone by Siaka Stevens, an ex-trade union leader, very left wing and incredibly corrupt.

"Siaka Stevens nationalised Sierra Leone Selection Trust (SLST), and it became the National Diamond Mining Company, but the government needed SLST to manage it, so SLST cut their losses and accepted a continuing holding of 45 per cent. Siaka Stevens was very close to Jamil Said Mohammed, the pre-eminent diamond dealer at that time, and together they ran what was left of the mine into the ground. Jamil subsequently bought part of the SLST holding, and eventually SLST sold out to the Precious Minerals Corporation."

Andy said "If you know anything about diamond mines, you know about the spread of stones: there is a distribution curve. If you see lots of smaller stones and then just a few larger ones with nothing in the middle range, you know stones have been stolen. We saw this happening with the diamonds from SLST, and eventually the company collapsed - there was too little money to keep it going."

"Interestingly, Mustapha used to say 'If you guys weren't here, I wouldn't want this job.' The phone would never stop ringing with people, including government officials, asking for a loan or whatever. Mustapha liked having expatriates around because he could say they were in charge. Yet he was perfectly able to do the job. He is no longer the manager; he is just the consultant. In the old days we managed the whole parastatal, but it is now run by a Sierra Leonean.

"The vast majority of our clients in terms of volume of diamonds were Lebanese. The family of one Lebanese man in particular had lived in Sierra Leone over several generations. This Lebanese man knew the country, the system, and the people all over the Eastern diamondiferous area. He alone accounted for a considerable percentage of the annual exports. His family would give large amounts of cash to Sierra

Leoneans to go upcountry to buy on their behalf, which required knowing the people and the terrain producing alluvial diamonds."

There is a diamond mining company called Koidu that a Sierra Leonean friend and the former Deputy Accountant-General, John Daramy knew well. John told me "During the war, the Sierra Leonean government had the support of a group of mercenaries called Executive Outcomes, who were South African and British. Mark Thatcher was rumoured to be an Executive Outcomes Director. They were funded by the UK government to the tune of about a million pounds a month to provide security for the Sierra Leonean government until the UK government objected to Peter Penfold, the High Commissioner, insisting that the Sierra Leone continued to need them otherwise the government would fall. Penfold was right, and Robin Cook, the then Foreign Secretary, resigned after rebels arrived in Freetown."

John continued "I knew all of the men as I would pay them their salaries. After the war, Union Trust Bank opened a branch in Koidu, and a friend who was a director invited me up for a weekend. He said we were having lunch with Koidu Holdings, the diamond people. He took me to their office and introduced me. By the time we got to the fourth person, we were all giggling as I knew everyone: they were all Executive Outcomes. So that was when I realised that once payments from the UK Government to Executive Outcomes had come to an end, the Kabbah government had signed an agreement with them - if they continued running security without payment, they could have Koidu Holdings.

"But this was a totally unreasonable and opaque agreement: the Sierra Leonean government had no control over the mine, and who knew how many diamonds came out of it. There were no Sierra Leonean sorters - they were all from Malaysia and Israel. Even the truck drivers were foreign. The last time I was in Sierra Leone in 2022 I met many of them. The name has changed but they are still the same people."

Andy resumed "Occasionally we'd get a stone from State House, which meant the President or Chief of Staff. On one occasion, we all looked at the diamond and said 'It's not real; it doesn't feel right.' The courier accepted our word, but as he was preparing to leave, I suddenly thought 'It doesn't feel right' was a hell of a weak-sounding explanation, even if it was actually true. So we sent someone after the courier to bring him back. We found a diamond tester and used that. A diamond is a very good conductor of electricity. The tester had an epi pen. Upon contact with the stone it turns green for diamond, red for anything else. So we told the guy, although it doesn't feel right, we can show you in this test that it isn't real. We did the test, and sure enough it turned red. So he could go back to the president and report back more convincingly.

"Naturally exporters wanted a low valuation so they would pay less tax on their parcels. We'd say we can do this in one of two ways: either you give us a realistic valuation or we can take all day to go through every single stone and set a value. The trick was that it was like going fishing: you don't want to set a high valuation which would be unfair. Don't forget, smuggling hadn't stopped there. You were trying to make the client feel safe coming to the office - that he would get a reasonable market value and a safe export procedure to board an aircraft.

"But if we said it was worth 100 when it was only worth 80, they would have to pay export duty on 100 only to be told in Antwerp it was only worth 80. If that happened, the client would rightly have felt he had been overtaxed. So the trick was to slightly undervalue parcels, so the clients were satisfied to the point that smuggling was not in their interests."

I put the question about smuggling in Sierra Leone after the Kimberly Process to Martyn, who replied "What Andy says is basically true. Kimberly resulted in the abolition of the extensive black market in rough diamonds, particularly in Antwerp. The benefit of smuggling became marginal. However, there was another major factor involved. After the fall of Jamil Said Mohammed, another firm run by the Mackie family built up a dominant position in the Sierra Leonean market. Their policy was to make a profit by turning over their capital several times a year rather than going for a big mark-up on purchases. As a result of this, sometimes prices appeared higher in Sierra Leone than Antwerp, so at least some of the new buyers hoping to make a killing in Sierra Leone found that their best bet was to return and sell their goods in Sierra Leone. Nevertheless, I am sure that a proportion of the production may still be smuggled - particularly large or fine goods - but it is only minimal."

But John Daramy believes there is still significant smuggling: "A lot of Sierra Leonean diamonds (over 50 per cent) never go through government export channels. Many are traded through Guinea and Gambia, where people are fabulously wealthy. I have relatives in the diamond industry with fantastic mansions in the Lebanon. I walked into an office in Bo where my extended relatives were, and I saw thousands of diamonds like one sees in movies on a salver in front of them. They operate by smuggling through Guinea and onto the Ivory Coast or wherever, but the trading starts a lot earlier.

"A few have export licences. They also have very good VHF radio systems. A Sierra Leonean would take diamonds to the Lebanese - say 1.5 carats. They would offer them something for the diamond, and haggle over it. The person would leave without selling, and the Lebanese would then get on VHF radio to all Lebanese so that they would all offer the same or a lower price. That's how they control it. It's a cartel. When they all give it to an export licence holder (a licence costs about $40K for a year), from their point of view it's good to pool it, so what comes out is shared. But only a minute quantity goes through the legal channels."

Andy's view on this was that yes, there are plenty of traders using diamonds. In countries with weak currencies and no reserve bank with foreign exchange, diamonds are a currency. The traders buy containers of goods - engine parts, rice, etc. - for which they have to pay in hard currency overseas. They sell to their clients in local currency. So how do they obtain hard currency for the next round of purchasing? They need a vehicle to take the money out and back into hard currency.

As to the question of whether they are selling diamonds illegally, there are two possibilities, and both revolve around the traders' interests in maintaining a low profile. In Sierra Leone they do not want it to be known that they are wealthy – that would pose a risk in terms of political pressure, taxation, etc. The first scenario is that they smuggle the diamonds into a neighbouring country and export through that country's channels, thereby maintaining their low profile in Sierra Leone. The second is that they go through no legal channels in any country and turn up in Antwerp to sell their diamonds. But diamonds without certification pose challenges to Antwerp buyers, who will therefore pay less because of the risk they are taking in case they get challenged by the authorities. So all options weighed up, it is still in the diamond sellers' interests to use legal channels, albeit in a second country, and pay the export duty.

I asked Andy "Were you ever threatened because you didn't do what someone powerful wanted you to do?"

"The only time I felt someone's wrath was while I was in Guinea. I'd valued some diamonds that morning, and when I went to the airport later I went through the scanner and they wanted to search my bags. So I said ok, fine, I'll turn out all my bags right here in the business lounge. Because obviously if I'd gone off to a private room somewhere, those guys could have planted a parcel of diamonds on me. Turning out my bags there and then stopped that from happening. I guess this was initiated by an unhappy client. But there were no actual threats from anyone.

"The civil war started after I'd been there a while. I think GGDO carried on in the first instance. I can't remember how that worked now. What I did see during the war was a young boy at the airport who was begging, and both of his hands had been chopped off. We'd always give him money. He was only a teenager at best.

"Another thing I remember about the war just says something very positive about Africans. At Lakka I'd set off to work and Mustapha lived on the way, so I stopped off as I'd heard there was shooting in town and Mustapha had heard there was shooting just 400 yards from the office. I drove back to the hotel, warning people along the way. The next morning, the same rebels came to the hotel. I could hear shooting nearby, and it was more like shooting for communication. I remember distinctly that the tannoy was playing Bill Hayley singing 'Rock around the Clock', and it seemed that the rebel firing was in time to the music. The French girls were all topless by the poolside, and I approached them and said 'I don't like to say this ordinarily, but there's a coup going on and I suggest you might want to cover yourselves up.'

"It was almost a ridiculous situation - you could imagine the tannoy announcing lunch would be served a little later. The rebels came into the hotel carrying guns. Pierre asked 'What do you want?' They said money and women. I think we both said find your own women, but we came up with some cash. They were happy with that. I remember one of them was eating a fried egg sandwich from the kitchen, and I said that looks like a really nice sandwich and he just tore it in half and gave it to me. It was funny because you'd have thought he might want to smash the face of a white man, but not at all.

"Things began to return to normal though the army rode around heavily armed. There was a soldier who used to sit on the spare wheel of a vehicle carrying two rocket-propelled grenades. What on earth he thought he was doing is anyone's guess. They used to travel around in convoy at speed. Anyway, I heard he fell off and the vehicle behind ran him over.

"We were asked to do a shipment for the NDMC (National Diamond Mining Company), which had been taken over from Sierra Leone Selection Trust. The army was hungry for cash so we went in on a Saturday. It was late afternoon, and I was driving back to the hotel afterwards. There was a particular fork in the road where a left turn took me back to the hotel, a right to the beach and bars. I decided on the right fork, and had gone a little way down the road when a Mercedes with soldiers on board cut across my vehicle. A soldier got out and ordered my passenger into the back. He then proceeded to load a revolver. He told me to drive up the hill to the Kabassa Lodge. This is a fortress-like residence built by one of the previous presidents, a monument in concrete. The place was crawling with soldiers. I was directed to one called Bio who was in his 20s. He was to become the Minister of Mines shortly afterwards. He asked about the NDMC shipment, carats, and value. I remember asking him to use his phone to call me about it next time!

"After a somewhat peaceful coup, the new government headed up by Valentine Strasser, aged 24, decreed a curfew. No one was to be away from home after 11pm. I was rolling back to the hotel with a couple of Lebanese friends. We had been drinking and were in top form. A huge snake was crossing the road. I'm not exaggerating when I say it was five foot or so long. So like any white hunter I drove over it a couple of times - death by Toyota Land Cruiser. Nabil decided to get out and pick it up. In his inebriated state, he missed the back of the head and got it further down the body. The snake was not quite dead, and turned its head and bit Nabil, who then proceeded to beat it to death. Panic set in. I was wondering where at 11pm in a town that was locked down, in curfew, you could find a doctor or hospital for help. We drove back to the hotel with the snake wrapped in death around his arm.

"Having sobered up quite quickly, we realised that this was a boa constrictor and so not actually poisonous. After washing the bite in whiskey, we all had another drink and coiled the snake up in the freezer for the cook to discover the following day.

"Near the hotel there was a bush bar disco. This was fun place to go where the music was loud and the beer cold. The problem was that so many people knew me that it could be expensive buying rounds. It had a stone dance floor and was packed as usual. At one end there was a smallish tree. Someone spotted a snake and was trying to dislodge it with a branch. There were three soldiers at the disco who decided to shoot the snake out of the tree. Everyone got back behind these guys, who proceeded to open up with their AK47s. There were shell casings everywhere and bits of the tree were flying off. The snake was fine. They must have fired 90 rounds into that tree. The funniest sight was a chap with a stick who somehow pulled back the branch, thereby catapulting the snake through the air. The crowd reared back in unison, like a wave at a football stadium. One soldier fell and the snake landed between his legs. I have never seen anyone get up so quickly.

"I was working in both Guinea and Sierra Leone at the time when Freetown was on the verge of being attacked, and a lot of people got out. Mustapha had applied for a visa to America, a green card, and he went down to the Mama Yoko Hotel, where there was a soldier on the roof firing at the rebels. The Americans came in having cordoned off both ends of the beach, and they got all the people in the hotel funnelled down onto the beach. They were taken out to a ship on the horizon, all protected by Apache helicopter. Mustapha was able to escape.

"Some weeks later in Guinea, I was buying lunch for some Sierra Leoneans I knew who had arrived there. When I saw Mustapha, I almost cried. I saw him off at the airport to America, and all he had was a plastic bag with a t-shirt in it. He was used to ordering his suits from Hong Kong - they would come and measure him, he would pay, and then the suits would be sent.

"The rebels took everything from the houses they occupied, including tiles off walls, and even removed the toilets. When Mustapha finally got his property back, I offered to lend him the money to rebuild his house. When he sold the house to a Jewish lawyer, Mustapha wired the money back to me immediately. He lived under a Moslem code, and he'd made a commitment so the loan had to be paid back. He is one of the most honest men I have ever met."

Andy went to Sierra Leone frequently over a period of almost 30 years. In that time, he became very familiar with dozens of international aid projects through knowing several of the Sierra Leoneans and foreigners who worked on them. I was interested to know his views on those aid projects given most foreign aid workers barely spend more than three to four years in any given country and so rarely if ever see the longer-term consequences of their aid projects.

He said "There was a workshop on the diamond industry after the civil war came to an end. The purpose was to jump-start the diamond business. It was run by someone from the American Embassy. About 20 or 25 people were invited, including some who represented the mines and the Ministry, and two who had been with De Beers, but no longer working there at the time. It was a workshop. There was a big table. There was a facilitator who presented herself and gave the purpose of the workshop. She told us to draw pictures of what the future might look like. I don't remember what the angle was, but it was ridiculous."

"Ha, that was the ice breaker," I chimed in. "You clearly weren't a workshop habitué."

Andy continued "At the time Foday Sankoh, the rebel leader who later went to jail, was initially made Minister of Mines to get the peace process underway. He didn't attend. The first thing I asked was 'Where are the Lebanese?' I was shouted down: 'They are not Sierra Leoneans.' I said 'Yes, but they are the backbone of your economy in diamonds and trading, so surely their voice is of value.' So that question was asked and answered."

Reflecting on Andy's story, it struck me that there were many important issues that this sort of workshop could and should have tackled. Given the government was responsible for tackling child and forced labour as part of its obligations as a signatory to dozens of International Labour Organisation conventions, it needed to engage with the Lebanese if it hoped to take any action. Over the years, there have been several reports about child and forced labour in Siera Leone and elsewhere. That said, Andy, Martyn and industry writer Chaim Even-Zohar consider many of these reports were exaggerated and that in communities surviving on subsistence farming, alluvial mining represented an important opportunity to support family livelihoods. I found one NGO report defined children as aged 9-17, which seemed a stretch of the notion of childhood when even ILO Convention C138 – Minimum Age Convention – specifies a minimum age of 15.

Andy said "The miners weren't using their own money. The Lebanese subsidised them. They gave them shovels, fed them, they gave them diesel generators to empty water from the pits, and then there was a sharing scheme to split the profits. And they paid them even when no diamonds were found in the pits. How do I know that? Because that's how it worked, because if you wanted some mining done you had to subsidise them, otherwise they would go back to farming.

"DFID also became quite involved – too involved – in the diamond industry. They appointed someone they referred to as a Diamond Tsar. Mustapha told me that a Dutchman came to 're-organise the industry.' He told us he was going to advise the government on how to run the diamond business. The strange thing was he didn't know anything about diamonds, but he insisted that our company, Diamond Counsellor International (DCI), was incompetent. He clearly didn't want DCI to win the upcoming tender for the GGDO post, and he even took the tender documents from the Ministry of Mines back to DFID in London, which seriously undermined the Sierra Leonean government. However, DCI won all the same because all the other bids were ridiculously high, and no one could compete with DCI's knowledge and expertise.

"It says something for Martyn Marriott's contribution to the diamond industry in Sierra Leone that he was awarded the Order of the Rokel, an award which recognises Sierra Leoneans who have distinguished themselves by making valuable contributions to the country in the areas of public service, arts, science, and philanthropy."

"Did you witness examples of corruption in Sierra Leone?" I asked.

"I have not seen real corruption at work, but I do remember an incident while I was staying at the Lakka Cotton Club hotel. There was a Dr (PhD) from the UN who wanted to run a workshop there with accommodation, meals, breaks, and entertainment. He asked Pierre for a quote for the workshop, and then a second to work in 0.5 million Leones for the doctor to pick up when he came to pay. Pierre wasn't surprised, but then no one was - that was the way it was. But I was surprised because it was a doctor from the UN, and he would have been paid a good salary. But if you remember the UN had a huge audit once over their travel department, and a lot of money had gone missing.

"A Canadian friend of mine ran an orphanage in Freetown. They had set up a print shop and they taught kids to run it. My friend said he fell out with a colleague when he (the Canadian) refused to sign off an invoice for $65,000 just to connect up a generator! There was a lot of palaver about it. I imagine back in those days they weren't so tight on auditing, so maybe the person back in the funding office in Germany had no idea what these things might cost in Sierra Leone. They would be seeing all sorts of inflated invoices all the time. You can't question every item.

"As for the special courts, it was a special circus. After the war came to an end, the International Criminal Court jumped in. They wanted to prosecute all and everyone, ideally in The Hague. The Sierra Leoneans were able to insist the trials took place in Freetown, and I think The Hague or the United Nations spent around $200 million building a special courthouse and special prison, all with electricity which of course the rest of Freetown did not have. Many Sierra Leoneans said if you have all this money, why didn't you put it into prosthetics for people who had limbs chopped off? But a lot of foreign lawyers had their CVs nicely pumped up as war crimes prosecutors, and a lot of Sierra Leoneans benefited from all the services that were required by the courts.

"The court cases went on for years. The judge got sanctioned for writing a book with the outcome before the end of the trial. The prosecutor didn't see it through till the end. A few of the just 13 men indicted died in prison before a judgement was reached. Foday Sankoh was there for a while. One story says that he tried to escape and was shot climbing over the wall. Another says he died in prison due to poor health.

"While this was going on, I'd say to the people in the office 'I want you to tell me the names of all 13 people being tried.' They couldn't. At the end, they'd spent a lot of money and I don't even know what the outcome was. The remaining ones found guilty were sent back to The Hague. The view of most Sierra Leoneans I spoke to was that they weren't interested, they didn't believe what they read in the newspapers, it had mostly happened upcountry, and they didn't know anyone."

John Daramy held a similar view: "Almost no one had heard of the people they arrested and charged. I remember one person who was supposed to be a spokesperson for Fodah Sankoh's rebel group. President Tejan Kabbah encouraged him to come forward because he was articulate, but the spokesman ended up being arrested and charged with crimes against humanity.

When Foday Sankoh was arrested, he was actually Vice-President at the time and was made Minister of Mines. The whole thing was rigged from start to finish, and they spent millions. There's another farcical story. There was a 110-year-old cotton tree outside the special court, and when they were building the court they decided to cut it down, but first they sent four consultants from the USA to investigate the whys and wherefores of the tree being cut down.

"I met up one day with a magistrate friend from Switzerland who told me she was going to give evidence the following day. I asked how she could give evidence? She said I've interviewed some of the child soldiers and I'm giving evidence on their part. I said in an English court that's hearsay because no one can cross-examine you. But although the children didn't go to prison, it was still wrong, flawed. Very few victims came from upcountry to give evidence."

Andy stayed friends with many Sierra Leoneans over the years, including Pierre the hotel owner until his death. He recounted wryly one story about his friend "You can get away with many things in Sierra Leone, but bigamy is not one of them. A Danish woman came to stay at Lakka in the dry season and formed a relationship with Pierre. During a rather drunken moment, Pierre proposed marriage to her and she accepted. I reminded Pierre that he was already married to a woman who had moved to America and whose father was a lawyer who loathed Pierre. However, when I returned to Freetown on one visit, I discovered they were married. They had presented themselves to a judge who, upon asking if there were any just impediments to the marriage taking place, had been told no.

"Pierre soon realised that his rush to marriage was likely to put him in jail as even in Freetown bigamy was somewhat frowned upon. Hasty letters and phone calls were made to barrister friends in London to courier divorce papers to number one wife in America. As you can imagine, number two marriage was also rather short, and sitting at the bar one day, Pierre received a letter in Danish. Fortunately there was a Dane sitting at the bar who read the letter and said 'Congratulations, you are divorced!'"

Chapter 11: Ethiopia and tales of NGOs

"Ann has a PhD in basket weaving."

Poking fun at my academic credentials was Andy's oblique way of congratulating me for being clever while not 'letting it go to my head'. The PhD in basket weaving once saved the day during an awkward meeting with academics from Addis Ababa University. The conversation descended into a bit of a brawl, and voices were raised as the professors boasted about who was the most senior among them, and who therefore knew best. When I announced with a certain irony the highfalutin' theme of my PhD, they burst into laughter and the tension was diffused.

For four years, I was Team Leader for a tiny project in Ethiopia, and had a chance to discover a little about a fascinating African country, the only nation which had never been colonised, and which had had a sizeable empire in the past and a ruler with the title of Emperor. Despite knowing quite a lot about Africa by then, I am ashamed to admit that my only knowledge of Ethiopia concerned the famine in the 1980s, and that was merely as a result of the Live Aid fundraising concerts.

The fossil skeleton remains of a human ancestor named Lucy were discovered in Hadar in Ethiopia in 1974, and until recently she was considered the oldest-known member of the human family. The former capital of Ethiopia, Axum, was originally the centre of the Axumite

Empire, which lasted around a thousand years, and spilled over into present-day Yemen, Saudi Arabia, Eritrea, Djibouti, northern Ethiopia, Sudan, and Somalia. In its day, it was considered as powerful a kingdom as those of Persia, China, and Rome. Ethiopians claim that God himself blessed this empire, based on the Kebra Negast (Glory of the Kings), the book which provides Ethiopia with its founding myth.

During the Cold War, Ethiopia gained considerable leverage over the international community by using the powerful weapon of collective guilt over its failure to support Ethiopia during Italian occupation. Haile Selassie, the last Emperor, had addressed the League of Nations in a moving speech "You owe us. You stood by and did nothing while Italy gassed our villages", but he had been ignored.

As the Cold War progressed, Haile Selassie persuaded the United States that Ethiopia could play a key role as a secondary line of defence that would keep Communism out of the area and guarantee Western access to the oil-rich Persian Gulf. Convincing America of Ethiopia's strategic importance helped ensure that Moscow reached the same conclusion.

As Michela Wrong put it "What made the Horn unique, and left it uniquely damaged, was that midway through the Cold War tango, the two dancing couples – Somalia and the Soviet Union in one corner, Ethiopia and the

United States in the other – separated, strode past each other on the ballroom and swapped partners."[48]

The Soviet Union poured nearly $9 billion in military hardware into Ethiopia, which corresponded to over $5,400 in weaponry for every Ethiopian citizen. In 1984 alone, Ethiopia imported about £1.2 billion in weapons, and that very year a serious famine occurred leaving a million people dead.

According to Bill Fraser, the Ethiopian government devoted 90 per cent of its budget to war, and it was left to aid agencies and Live Aid to help feed starving Ethiopians. At the time, Bill contributed regularly to Save the Children, and had a call from them asking him for an extra contribution. His response was a curt one "No. The Ethiopians are deliberately using the aid to fund the army. That's not my fault. It's their decision."

He had a call back from a senior person in Save the Children, who said they hadn't realised what was happening. This was because the Save the Children staff in Ethiopia didn't want to relay this inconvenient truth to their headquarters for fear that the money would stop as would their jobs.

My project office was on the Bole Road, one of the busiest roads in Addis Ababa, lined with office blocks and restaurants. Our building had an excellent and reliable restaurant, the Stockholm, on the ground floor, where we would go for lunch and even hold some meetings given the office itself was only one room. Across the road was the Limetree restaurant, which had a bookshop, excellent food including a Mongolian stir-fry once a week, and the odd very healthy food option such as shots of extremely sour wheatgrass. Next door was a small gym, set up by the double Olympic gold medallist runner Haile Gebrselassie, who would often be training on a bike right next to me. While I was cycling slowly on an uphill programme, Gebrselassie would be zooming along at five times my speed!

I spent every other month in Addis Ababa, and because I was not expected to work at the weekends, this was a time to explore. The country was not yet very developed from a tourism perspective, but there were a few tour operators, and accommodation and travel were variable feasts and experiences, but at least they were free from the clutches of Trip Advisor and similar travel sites. Most of my visits were organised by a New Zealander who had travelled the entire world and come to the conclusion that Ethiopia was the most fascinating country of all. She decided to stay and set up a small tour company.

On one occasion, an Australian friend, her son and I walked and travelled by mule from the ancient city of Lalibela up to a tiny hamlet on a plateau atop a mountain at around 3,000 metres altitude. We arrived wet and freezing cold, with only a small fire to try to dry ourselves and our clothing. I was offered a room in a sort of small dormitory where the bed linen felt damp and the only 'bathroom' facility was an actual toilet in the middle of a large bramble bush. It was neither terribly accessible nor private. I opted instead for a smaller room with an outdoor toilet set on a sort of throne with a roof. The following morning, I awoke to sunshine and a loo with a view, looking out beyond the plateau to mist lying in the valley and mountain peaks in the near and far distance.

On other trips, we would walk for hours up into the mountains to see an ancient rock-hewn church, decorated with frescos and old rugs. Every church in Ethiopia contained a replica of the tablets in the Ark of the Covenant, but the original Ark is claimed by the Ethiopian Orthodox Church in Axum. Inside the Chapel of the Tablet, the Ark of the Covenant is guarded by an elected priest who stays there from the moment of his election to this highly privileged position until his death. The story goes that the priest wears a chain around an ankle so that the day when food that has been left for him on a tray outside the door remains uneaten, he is dragged out by the chain, thus ensuring that no other person ever enters the chapel. Upon his death, a new guardian is elected and he continues this solitary life of guardianship. Such selfless devotion was humbling.

Another visit to Axum brought us into contact with a Harrison Ford lookalike, an American archaeologist who had made an amazing chance discovery of a small burial chamber just outside the town. On reversing his vehicle, one of the back wheels had sunk into quite a deep hole, which turned out to be above a far deeper crater below. Harrison junior was persuaded to be lowered by rope into this hole, and deep down he found an ancient settlement the size of several football pitches.

Haile Selassie had lived in exile in England when his country was occupied by Italian fascist forces in the 1930s. One of his greatest supporters was Sylvia Pankhurst, best known as a pioneering suffragette. Sylvia's son Richard had moved with his mother and wife-to-be Rita to Ethiopia, and I met Richard and Rita one day at the Alliance Française, a French cultural institution. Richard had worked tirelessly for years through diplomatic channels to ensure that Ethiopia recovered one of its most iconic monuments, the Axum Obelisk, which had been taken to Rome, and it was eventually handed back - with difficulty given its immense size and weight. It was 24.6 metres high, and its 160 tons of funeral stele had to be cut into three sections. The return of the Axum Obelisk brought to an end the almost 70-year dispute over a symbol of African civilisation stolen by European troops as a war prize. Richard was not in the best of health by then, but Rita was charming and vivacious, and I plucked up the courage to ask if I could paint their portrait.

I painted many people in Ethiopia, and had the good fortune to be able to exhibit 20 or so paintings in Sidama Lodge, where I used to stay. The Lodge put on an annual exhibition in support of Ethiopian artists, and it gave me immense pleasure to be able to give portraits to people I had known or worked with over the years. In what is probably a rather sad reflection, I think I would rank these gifts as one of the most satisfying things I did in that fascinating country.

Andy came to stay with me on a few occasions to break up the long periods we spent apart. He would spend much of his time by the swimming pool at the Sheraton Hotel where he discovered much about life in Ethiopia which fell outside my narrow project purview. There were many Americans staying there who were in the process of adopting Ethiopian children. It turned out that Ethiopia was one of the biggest source countries for international adoption by US citizens until the practice was banned in 2018 on the grounds of potential abuse and human trafficking. He would often join me and my Ethiopian colleagues for lunch. They enjoyed his company because he had no truck with aid jargon and well meaning initiatives. As they laughed along with him, I could see they agreed with many of his views which were outlandish by mainstream aid standards. It was good to have him there and helpful to have his advice at times about sensitive issues which came up on this and a later project.

The project itself, which was tiny by the standards of the time – spending about £250,000 or so a year – originally came into existence with a "high importance" label attached to it. The Ethiopian government had introduced a law to register and restrict the kinds of activities which civil society organisations (CSOs) could carry out. In particular, it restricted CSOs from working on human rights, democracy and justice matters unless they were mainly funded locally. Another significant restriction was that no CSO should spend more than 30 per cent of its funds on administration, which was broadly defined: a minimum of 70 per cent must reach the target audience. The government wanted them to focus on providing services in the main sectors of health, education, etc., as well as humanitarian assistance.

In an interview with the BBC's HardTalk on April 2, 2009, Prime Minister Meles Zenawi responded to the challenge that the CSO Law undermined the independence of civil society by saying "It does not undermine the independence of Ethiopian civil society organisations. What it undermines is the funding of civil society organisations in Ethiopia who are involved in political activities from foreign sources. And I believe the practice in all developed countries is that political activities are funded from local sources."

Most interest in civil society organisations on all sides in the aid debate centres around the big charities, also called NGOs, which include household names such as Oxfam and Save the Children, rather than a broader notion of civil society, which extends to a wide range of groups, including trade union organisations, the media, various professional economic, social, medical societies, and membership associations such as football clubs, right down to small community-based organisations.

It seems that most overviews of aid significantly underestimate the amounts channelled through NGOs. In 2019, Manchester University researchers found that over half the 2015 UK overseas aid budget was spent through NGOs. The information seems ridiculously hard to come by, and the researchers had to trawl through a database they themselves had created of 895 NGOs in the UK. Donations from the public have been by far the most important source of funds for UK development NGOs, contributing nearly £10 billion over five years and 40 per cent of the sector's total income over this period.[49]

A similar picture is found in other countries. Comparing the average annual expenditure of Canadian NGOs (2011–2015) with Canadian development assistance in 2015 shows this to be the equivalent of more than 60 per cent of Canadian overseas development assistance.

I remember being amazed by how much funding the larger charities in Ethiopia received. One that stands out in my mind is Save the Children, which had an annual budget of $120 million a year, just for that one country alone.

Over the years, it often struck me that there was less pressure on NGOs to account for all their spending and activities. Many of the larger international NGOs received "accountable grants" at the time, for which they put forward a plan for their activities for a few years and requested a corresponding budget. Not a huge amount of detail was provided. When I held a few short-term consultancy posts as an Advisor in DFID, I was sometimes asked to do a "light touch" review of their annual reports: I was just to read them and highlight anything which was unclear or perhaps required additional checking.

Bill once told me "DFID simply thought of NGOs as some sort of unsophisticated outfits who were run by sandal wearing hippies who didn't have the time or skill to do book keeping."

By contrast, the private sector companies which won competitive tenders had to account for every single penny spent. Although rules varied slightly with greater or lesser flexibility, at times I would have to account for every bottle of water, taxi ride or sandwich, then photocopy the receipts and send copies together with my invoice. One of my bosses once said to me it rather seemed as if the NGOs had the luxury and latitude of unaccountable grants.

The major donors in Ethiopia, who had created a club called the Development Assistance Group (DAG), took the position that they were outraged that the Ethiopian government intended to impose limits on NGO activities. As time wore on, I had plenty of reasons to grow sceptical that this group's position constituted anything other than posturing, given NGOs are a fairly influential lobby in many of the group's countries and they needed to keep them sweet. Maybe there was a slightly neocolonialist attitude in their grandstanding along the lines of "we are in charge and we know what is best."

I suspect I was a bit of a wolf in sheep's clothing for this job. From my early experience of NGOs in Guinea onwards, I had harboured a certain scepticism. There were always several outstanding examples, such as Development Workshop in Angola, but there were plenty of others that fell far short in terms of their behaviour.

By the time I started working in Ethiopia, the massive increase in the UK aid budget had resulted in larger sums being handed over to the big NGOs, and there was increasing 'intermediation' – meaning several stages of actors involved in an aid distribution chain – between them and their NGO partners in developing countries.

Most of the large donor organisations in Ethiopia were running NGO grant operations through a large fund. The fund management was put out to tender, and it would usually be won by a private sector company with a strong background in auditing rather than civil society organisations. Fund management companies would award grants to NGOs through competitive local tenders.

In the past, NGOs had received direct core funding from aid agencies and wealthy individual donors, and many continued to do so, but there was increasing pressure on them to bid for grants. To do so, they needed a growing staff of researchers, finance, monitoring, and administrative officers to write bids and provide robust proof that they were able to guard against fiduciary risk, meaning to prevent the funds from being embezzled. All this obliged them to move away from the model of small operations run on a shoestring with committed staff working directly with local communities to improve local services and empower the poor. NGOs were starting to look, act, and sound like the big private consulting companies they so often derided.

In my experience, it is Africans and people from other developing countries who are most sceptical towards NGOs. The tree-hugging and tie-dyed-skirt-wearing foreign aid workers – as Andy is wont to call them – tend to be whole heartedly in favour of NGOs.

Two experts on Africa, Patrick Chabal and Jean-Pascal Daloz, claimed that the massive expansion in NGOs was the result of successful adaptation to the conditions laid down by foreign donors on local political actors who seek to gain access to new resources.[50] This was chapter and verse the argument put to me by Cherif Diallo in the World Bank back in Guinea. Another expert wrote that one of the reigning jokes in contemporary Nigeria is that when students complete their education, they have two options besides likely unemployment: founding a "new breed church" or starting a non-governmental organisation. Both are fertile grounds for corruption.[51]

John Daramy from Sierra Leone said "One of my biggest bugbears while I was Deputy Accountant-General, was

NGOs that would come in and present a project, which I had to sign off. They said they wanted to bring in say seven vehicles duty-free – an exemption permitted to NGOs in this and many countries – and I had to approve it. It was the same with salaries: they wanted salaries to be tax exempt. Obviously they all followed the same formula.

"The money for NGOs never went through the government channels. I used to argue with them forcefully that they were not actually helping the country. They would come in and say they wanted to do something in health and the government basically would wash their hands of it and let the NGOs do health. This made the government lazy, taking responsibility out of its hands. I'd say to them 'Name one country where you've been for five years, made a difference, and then left because the work was done.' None could give an example except Medecins Sans Frontiers.

"They were always looking for ways to spend more money even when it was clearly a waste, and ways to spread their messages far and wide. Someone came up with the bright idea of printing posters in the different Sierra Leonean local languages. Some of us pointed out that the target audience was 80 per cent illiterate and those who were educated in English could barely read the posters they made in Krio, but that didn't stop them employing language experts!"

Although I came to feel critical towards NGOs in general, especially the large ones, I remained enthusiastic and optimistic about many individual NGOs, especially some of the smaller ones who ran small-scale projects. A veteran of Citizen Advice Bureaux in the UK, Gil had worked in Ethiopia for many years, supporting projects in the broad area of human rights, and had started to identify individual Ethiopians with the necessary skills and commitment to work with her. Some worked in small Ethiopian charities which, according to them, were targeted by the Ethiopian legislation which clamped down on civil society because they were an effective challenge. She told me "It was a difficult time, around 2011, when I got funds from DFID, the Civil Society Challenge Fund. Our project was going to run Rights Advice Centres. Basically it was my Citizens Advice Bureau-type operation in Ethiopia. The original NGO whom I was to work with was caught out by the legislation, and its mandate became illegal.

"We then had to find a new home for our project, which had only just got underway. One of our team came up with the idea that if we went into partnership with the university, this would be deemed acceptable as it was a government body that could accept foreign money. I went to see the head of the Human Rights Centre in Addis University. He was very nice and agreeable, but said we still needed to get the President's say-so. I was wheeled in to meet this brandy-swilling, cigar chain-smoking guy in his office, a member of the EPDRF political party and immensely charming. And he took a shine to me! We hit it off and he signed on the dotted line. So that project went ahead."

In the various encounters I had with NGOs in Ethiopia, I was particularly impressed by Tearfund, which provided some support and training to self-help groups in Ethiopia. These groups were originally modelled on savings groups in India with a difference. The idea behind them was that poor people have untapped potential to help themselves but a small amoung external support could be very helpful. Tearfund provided a little training to these groups. One study calculated that for every $1 of donor support, the return or benefits ranged between $200 and $300. The Director of Tearfund said to us "We don't want any more more funding for the self-help groups because it could change their nature for the worse."

The Development Assistance Group (DAG) decided that they would have a project to track the trends in civil society in Ethiopia following the implementation of this law, which was to be funded by the British, Irish, and Dutch governments but answerable to all 26 DAG members. Atos won the tender and the project got underway. We were essentially one full-time Ethiopian officer, a part-time Team Leader (me), and two other team members with occasional inputs. We were fortunate to have a brilliant Director, whose 5 per cent of time given to this project was, at her own instigation, entirely elastic. The project rented a small unfurnished room in an office block, and we inherited a second-hand photocopier. We worked on our own laptops and used my colleague Gemechu's car to attend meetings, or took the cheap and cheerful blue taxis.

By the time we had won the contract and had "feet on the ground", the DAG had already lost interest. I suspect their key performance indicator on the Ethiopian government's restrictive law was simply something along the lines of "project tracking trends in civil society in Ethiopia commissioned." After the first month or so of operations, we were invited by the head of DFID to lunch with a couple of representatives of a British NGO. The DFID Head of Office spent the whole lunch in endless conversation with the NGO guys. At the end, as we were getting up to leave, he turned to me and asked with a false smile on his face "So in a word, how is the project going?"

I replied "In a word, fine." He had the grace to look a little sheepish, and apologised for not having more time to talk about it, whereupon he left.

As I had originally discovered in Guinea and elsewhere, civil society organisations and especially the NGOs had mushroomed. There had been none in Ethiopia during the period of the military Derg regime which ended in 1991, but 18 years later about 4,000 organisations were registered.

Our Research Director was an academic from Addis Ababa University, and we commissioned extensive research on understanding who the CSOs were, what they did, and how the law affected them. We brought in other academics from a range of social sciences at the university as well as a prestigious policy thinktank, itself a CSO, the Forum for Social Studies.

By the end of the project, we had amassed a huge inventory of information, data, and analysis of Ethiopian civil society, and had made – or so our academic colleagues told us entirely unprompted - a significant contribution to the country's understanding of all these organisations.

We were delighted with this praise, because the four years had been a hard slog negotiating the various positions and interests of the 26 DAG members, which ranged from those who probably really didn't care about the NGO law because their main interest in the country was security and their presence in the wider region (America being number one) to the Scandinavian agencies who really did care about human rights and wanted the NGOs they funded to be able to act upon human rights abuses. The British lay somewhere in between, generally taking a pragmatic position. They persuaded us to also offer to 'build capacity' - for which read influence and change views – in the government authority set up to register and monitor all CSO activity. This was all very well, and it certainly gave us some influence and a privileged seat at government and donor dialogue meetings, but it made quite a number of NGOs suspicious of us, and unwilling to collaborate in our research.

The main result of our project was that we did persuade the Ethiopian government to modify aspects of the NGO law, making it easier for them to operate. By taking the Civil Society Authority staff on trips to visit charities and see what they did and how they operated, we started to see a change in their views, so that they were gradually willing to modify certain aspects of the regulations, and they started to agree to legal exemptions for certain organisations.

Then, in 2019, the government enacted a new law to supersede the 2009 one. The new law modified many of the most contentious and challenging regulations, including the funding aspect. We cannot state that this radical change was entirely due to our project, but it certainly played an important role, or so our Ethiopian colleagues claim. More recently, the Civil Society Authority's Director General stated "We have been working hard to change the hostile relationship which existed between the former government and civil societies into constructive partnership by rendering services based on best practices such as transparency, accountability, and participation."[52]

Overall, I cannot help but feel that our little project had a major impact on understanding what civil society could do well, and changing the attitude of the Ethiopian government towards their role in development.

Chapter 12: Daring deeds and scandal in Angola

Andy's consultancy work with the Marriotts took him to Angola as well as Sierra Leone. The Angola experience marked the end stages of his working life in Africa, whereas when our paths crossed there I was just midway through my working life.

After I had started working in Angola in the early 2000s, I discovered that my diamond industry friend from Guinea days, Bob, was living there. One evening Bob and his friends invited me to go with them to a party in a flat inside one of the many dreary Soviet-built apartment blocks, which look not dissimilar to typical run-down council flats in any British city. A colleague of his was asked to pick me up at the Continental Hotel, and he in turn asked his friend, Andy Ward, to drop into the foyer to find me.

"Toby said 'she will be there, she's tall and blond.' When I saw you, I thought you looked familiar, but couldn't remember where I'd seen you before," Andy tells me.

"Did we chat at that party?" I asked.

"No, your sights were set on finding yourself an oil magnate."

"Ah yes, of course."

At lunch with Bob one day, someone in the oil industry commented on how remarkable it was that De Beers had put together a cadre of people like him to buy diamonds in remote parts of Africa. Like me, he felt these diamond buyers were paid quite modest salaries in relation to the huge risks and responsibilities they assumed and it appeared they were mostly trustworthy in the face of considerable temptation to steal. A couple of Bob's stories provided sobering examples:

"In Cafunfu, I was running a station and I could sense something wasn't right. We had lost control of our own security. It was run by an external company, and I wrote this in my handover note. At least 20 to 30 guards on each station had guns. Money was brought up to the station one day. The Angolan guards hated the British guard, who was mildly racist towards them. They beat the shit out of him, tied him up, stole all the money, and were on their way to the airport when they were caught by the military, who killed some of them and then handed us back about $100, saying 'That's all we could find.' And that was the end of that one.

"The serious one was in Lucapa. A plane carrying money with guards and three buyers on board arrived at the airstrip. Inka [Bob's girlfriend] was supposed to come up on the flight too, but she didn't in the end. They set off from the airport in a two or three car convoy with the money. One buyer, Ken, travelled in the money car with armed men, which we were always told we should never do. My driver had arranged for an ambush with the police and the military. They shot our men at very close range with AK47s. Ken got hit seven times and another man twice, but at such close range the bullets went straight through their bodies, fortunately without hitting any vital organs.

"We were waiting for them at the station, wondering what had happened. They were late. One vehicle eventually arrived and Ken stumbled out, a bloody mess. A doctor came up from the Lucapa mine to help. The other buyers had been kidnapped, beaten up, threatened, and tossed out along the road. One of them, Mark, had been in the New Zealand Special Forces. He had tried to flag down at least three UN vehicles for help, but none deigned to stop. Eventually someone gave them a lift. We stripped Ken's clothes off and Mark applied tourniquets to his wounds. Ken shouted out 'my balls', and Mark said 'Sorry, mate, they've gone!' Then he relented, 'Don't worry, mate, only joking, there they are!' We had no strong painkillers for Ken, and I remember trying to drown out the sound of his screaming throughout the night.

"We then spent three days arguing with the police, who threatened to shoot us. De Beers arranged to send two planes, one for medevac and the other for the rest of us. I asked my nominal boss, Neal, what we should do about the diamonds. He replied 'Fuck the diamonds, I don't give a shit about them – we're getting out of here!'

"This irked me, though I didn't blame him because he was probably in shock. I insisted 'No, we're not doing that. We've spent weeks buying them, and that will be the first thing Oppenheimer will ask you about.'

"So I was the one who managed to get the diamonds out. Playing a trick from Guinea, I picked the diamonds up, put them in a duffel bag and said 'You guys go in the first two armed vehicles, and I'll sit in the open-backed vehicle behind with Mark carrying a pistol across from me.'

"That night we drove to Lucapa airstrip. As the others were piling into the medevac plane, I walked up to the other plane without any security guards and with about £6 million worth of diamonds on me. I handed them to Mark to ensure they got back to London."

"But why did you take such a risk? What spurred you on? A sense of adventure?" I asked him.

"I didn't do it for pleasure, I was generally scared, but our job was to buy diamonds and I didn't fuck around. I was just going to do my job. There was no point in leaving the diamonds in the office. I would probably do the same again today.

"I opted to stay behind, because I hadn't been affected by it. Remember, I hadn't been in those cars. The two buyers flew back to London and were lauded as heroes for getting the diamonds out. I left ten days later, but they forced me to go back to Angola again. Someone pointed out that for each bullet you take in the British Army, you get paid out a lot more than you would taking a bullet for De Beers. And they even threatened to withhold Ken's pension because he shouldn't have been travelling in the car with the armed guards."

I would run across Andy's boss, Martyn Marriott's son Luke, from time to time over the next four years. Luke was always charming, and would ask me to call him the next time I was in town. I called twice on other visits, but each time another voice answered the office mobile and told me he was out of the country. Having plenty of other fish to fry, I didn't feel a great urge to keep trying, and I hovered in my mind over whether to put in a third call. The voice at the end of the line was the same as on the previous two occasions, but this time we talked and he, Andy, said "Luke's not here, but why don't you come out to dinner with me?"

For the only time in our 20 or so years together, we were both working in the same country. Over the course of a year, I met some of his colleagues and began to learn a little about what he did, which in comparison to me seemed to be 'sweet Fanny Adams'.[53] As I was emerging from a meeting in a hotel one day, Andy hailed me from the bar. "Are you free for lunch? We've just got some work to do, but we'll be done in five minutes."

Over the next five minutes, I witnessed the most extraordinary meeting. The question "What have you got?" went around the group. Answers ranged between 57 and 64. Andy said "So do we agree on 61?" An affirmative response all around, and lunch was ordered.

The numbers – in millions - represented the valuations of all the main parties to the next diamond negotiation. This rather short discussion was the pre-negotiation stage, which actually belied a lengthier, more complex process that I learnt about later. But it meant nothing to me at the time, and I left after lunch with an unwarranted sense of resentment over the comparison with my own heavy workload.

Angola would not be anyone's first choice of country to start dating. There were rather few good restaurants and clubs, and the roads were busy day and night so an evening's outing was usually not an option. We would spend weekends at a beach restaurant called Coconuts on the Ilha (island) just opposite the city or go with a group of the oil industry crowd further south to other beaches. One day we were in Luanda on the seafront when the city was celebrating Carnival. It was a grey, overcast day, the costumes were the most unexciting, unimaginative ones I had ever seen, and the atmosphere was pretty subdued. I remember noticing a young boy dressed in an oversized nappy holding a huge fake mobile phone. This was not Venice Carnival, and certainly not Rio de Janeiro, by any stretch of the imagination.

On one of my working visits, I moved in with Andy when he was staying in one of the more comfortable company/home offices. The garden had a small lawn and plunge pool. One weekend we decided to do a little gardening and bought some of the bougainvillea plants which were to be found everywhere in the city, magnificent in their vibrant pinks, reds and oranges. However, we managed to find the only non-flowering bougainvillea in the city, which took some doing. Or the problem was the gardener, who watered the tiny garden to such an extent that the small newly planted bougainvillea were washed down the street. Luke wanted to sack the gardener, but in the end decided to pay him more to come less often.

In the diamond working environment, everyone spoke English so Andy did not have to learn Portuguese, and even outside of work he could still communicate quite effectively. This point, I had to admit, was proved rather spectacularly one Saturday. Andy was sitting alone in the company house watching television when a shower of small stones struck the bars on the windows. A heavier barrage followed. Feeling thoroughly disgruntled, he got up and went outside to look for the guard, whom he found hiding crouched down on his seat by the gate with the door locked from the inside. Andy shouted at the guard in English "What's going on? Open up that gate immediately!"

Shamefaced, the guard unbolted the latch and opened the door. Outside there were no kids, small or large, causing the disturbance, and instead, Andy came face to face with a diminutive young woman. He shouted "What the hell are you doing?" Realising he didn't speak Portuguese, the woman whipped up her top, squirted breast milk at him, and proceeded to make the international symbol for money with one hand while pointing at the guard with the other.

"I understood the situation perfectly," he recounts confidently. "I shouted at the guard to pay the woman, yelled at her to stop throwing stones, and then resumed my position in front of the television set."

My third offer of marriage came at this time with the gift of a diamond for an engagement ring, a fancy intense yellow stone. No blood had been wiped off it! Andy's friend in Angola, Leon, was quick to say "How lovely. I recall David Beckham gave a yellow diamond to his wife after he betrayed her." Andy fired back with "if that were the reason for a yellow diamond, I would have given Ann a whole string of them." I doubt I am the typical diamond geezer wife but the emotional significance of this stone touched me deeply, coming from a man I had come to appreciate as a loving and caring partner, son and father – despite his protestations to the contrary due to his long absences from home. On another occasion, I turned down the offer of a beautiful pair of diamond ear-rings. He had suddenly presented them to me in a fancy case as I was getting dressed for his friend's wedding. It felt like a scene out of the film Pretty Woman when Julia Roberts receives a choker of hearts set with diamonds and rubies. I wore the ear-rings for the wedding. They were on loan from Luke Marriott's jewellery shop and I could either keep them or return them to the shop the following week because Andy was flying back to Angola. I took them back to the shop.

I came to understand that Andy hated Angola and hated the work, and I didn't envy him the long hours and days of doing nothing, often alone in the office house. The situation in the industry had changed substantially since Martyn Marriott had first won the contract. In those days, valuations were important to establish a reserve price for the tenders, and considerable efforts were made to ensure Angola got a fair market price.

Martyn had said to me when we met "During the lull after losing the Botswana contract, I had contacted Diamang, the state diamond enterprise in Angola, in January 1985. Nothing came of this till I suddenly got a telex from them in December asking me to come to Luanda for discussions. It was arranged that they would meet me at the airport, and off I went only to find no welcome and so I had to fly straight back home. There was a flurry of apologetic telexes and urgent pleas for me to return, and a few days before Christmas I was appointed diamond consultant to the government.

"Angola's production was small, so believing that it could do no damage to the De Beers' Central Selling Organisation monopoly, I advised them to sell it on tender in Antwerp. Initially it was sold to a single Antwerp merchant, but eventually they agreed to a tender, and the Angolans insisted the tender had to take place in Luanda. I set about persuading a group of Antwerp diamond dealers to fly in for it, but mindful of the chances of their forming a ring I included Jacques Graubart, a great friend of Milos', in the group.

"The tender took place and, surprise, surprise, all the dealers' bids came in a cluster around 20 per cent below our valuation. I reported this to the new Managing Director, Noe Baltazar, but he was unsurprised because it transpired the Angolans had all the buyers' hotel rooms bugged, and knew exactly what was going on. He asked me to select the buyer most likely to break the ring, and I chose George Evens, who then bought the goods at our price. Graubart, having betrayed us, was furious! It was a friend lost.

"Another incident from the early days in Angola: initially we were asked to value the goods at the mine for security reasons. As a result, Peter and I had to conduct a valuation in Andrada in the far north of the country. It was quite scary. The civil war was still going strong. To land at the airport, the plane had to descend in tight circles to avoid enemy fire. All went well, and we got back to Luanda. The next day UNITA captured the mine and marched all the expatriate staff hundreds of miles south to their base there as hostages. It was a narrow escape!

"We had a whole string of tenders in Angola. The country was immensely corrupt, though hadn't been when we started. The former President José Eduardo dos Santos' famous daughter Isabel, promoted by one of the major diamond dealers, saw a possibility so pressure was put on, and the price of diamonds went down and down and down. By that stage, my son Luke was doing the valuations, but he pulled out and said 'I can't do this any more.' We had a very good young Angolan, André Buca, who went along with everything in our name and did it all. But nothing changed; we simply went through the motions."

Andy described the selling process to me: "People were invited by Sodiam, the marketing arm of Angola Endiama, a parastatal, to buy the diamonds. The negotiations were something of a pantomime. They consisted of the buyer, a valuer from the mines, an independent valuer – us – and Sodiam. Each representative would value the diamonds over the course of a week, and then there would be a lot of after-hours horse-trading over how bad the market was, etc. Then we would go through the charade of the negotiation as if it weren't already known what the buyer would pay.

"I took two of those Comic Relief red noses to Angola and told my friend Leon that we should wear them during the negotiations. Leon was horrified. Obviously this would have been hugely disrespectful. While we were negotiating, I looked meaningfully across at him and then lowered my hand and made as if to pick up a red nose, which I pretended to place on my nose. Leon was beside himself, trying to keep a straight face.

"In these sorts of things, no one wants to rock the boat, and stupidly the people who lose are the mines. If the mines lose, they go out of business and are unable to do any new exploration. A lot of mines would go out of business in Angola, and then new investors would come in. During the war, all the fuel had to be flown up to the mines so you can imagine the cost of that alone. Now they can drive the fuel up, but on perilously dangerous roads.

"The thing was that everything was arranged. That's why no one liked Angola tenders, because everyone knew what the price would be before the envelopes were open. It was wonderful for the buyers - a good profit in the rough, and back home they could divide up the diamonds into smaller more saleable categories to maximise their profits. But don't forget, they had to pay off lots of people to get there, including Endiama, the Minister of Mines, the President, and the President's daughter.

"There was an incident with a new guy from South Africa, a mine valuer. He wouldn't agree on the price. The head of Endiama or Sodiam came in and said to him 'If you can't come up with a price, we will.' And they stalked out again.

"Invariably the mines needed the money to run the mine and pay their staff, so they could not refuse the sale price. They had insufficient working capital so they couldn't hold back the shipment and mix it in with the next one. They were mining 'hand to mouth'. One South African said 'It cost me more to get these diamonds out of the ground than this sale price.'

"'So leave them in the ground,' I said. They did pay export taxes on them, but that was Endiama's role rather than ours, unlike in Sierra Leone. Don't forget, it was a big operation. They would have had export licences and Kimberly certificates, so from that side it was all legitimate. The deals took place beforehand."

One day, Andy was accused of stealing a diamond. It seemed a bizarre quirk of fate that both he and my father should be accused of the same thing. He told me the story: "There is a stock control handling. On this occasion it was a Catoca shipment. You couldn't afford the time to look closely at every stone. There were three people looking at the shipment of specials of Catoca. One of them told me 'There's one large stone missing.' I said that's ok, we'll deal with it when it comes to the end. It was probably my fault for not weighing it all up. Leon had looked at the diamonds before me - he was the mines valuer - and he told me which stone was missing. Although it was a stone of no real value, all hell broke loose. Somebody had set me up, because no one steals a stone like that. I couldn't even see the point of stealing it, apart from using it as a pretext to get rid of someone.

"I offered to be strip-searched immediately but oh no, that wasn't accepted. So who knows what happened. They never found it. It went into somebody's pocket and left the building. I was suspended and so was the last guy to hand me the parcel, but he on full pay. Later he went back to work, but I was never invited back.

"This sort of unsubstantiated allegation could have been highly detrimental to the Marriotts, DCI, and myself. But give me some credit: if I were going to steal a stone, it wouldn't be this 20-carat piece of junk. However, it all worked out in the end because the Marriotts never doubted me for a second, and I hated the place anyhow.

"It had been very different when Martyn and Peter used to go to Angola in the early days. They were lauded and shown respect. But as time went on, the Angolans got cocky and felt they didn't need us any more. I remember the funniest thing there, at lunch at the Endiama office. I had a plate, and the woman serving called me and asked me to give her my plate. I thought thanks, expecting she would serve me food, but not at all - she filled my plate and gave it to someone else. That's how much things had changed. Martyn would have sat down and been served lunch with a linen napkin.

"Another great scam was that in Angola it was customary to give and receive 'calabash' (gifts). The Endiama/Sodiam Director of Finance would hand out Christmas boxes full of wine, food, and other gifts. She would fly to Portugal to buy Rolex watches, new Range Rovers, and the like. Every year there would be another car. How much she claimed on top of the cost, who knew."

Commenting on the negotiations over the sale of diamonds, Bob said "In Angola, De Beers still had the monopoly till about 2000 so up till then everyone relied on and knew De Beer's pricing system. After the peace accords, there were only a few companies operating and they would all fly out to Angola for the negotiations. If they got near the price, that was acceptable. So there was nothing crooked about it. The crookedness came in after the very wealthy Israelis and Russians arrived on the scene. Those guys wanted to make money. But we were still ok till the 2008 financial crash, and that hit the diamond industry really hard. Sales dropped by 60 per cent and then rebounded after seven or eight months. From that point on, they really put the screws on.

"From 2002 to 2008, we – the mining companies who had done all the hard work - were probably about 30 per cent below the real price before costs and taxes were taken off. After 2008, we sold for even less. In effect, although the diamonds were sold at market price, the mines suffered because they were obliged to make up the payments to corrupt officials."

I asked "What about the government share of revenue?"

"They didn't give a toss, because they wanted their action then and there. Who knew if they would be kicked out tomorrow? You had to make the most of 'your turn to eat'.[54] The big thing about diamonds is that the sales are all done in US dollars, so very useful."

At this time, Angola was awash with scandal at the highest levels. A judicial case in France involved arms sales to Angola during the 1993-2000 civil war worth US$790 million by a French businessman, Pierre Falcone, and his Russian-born associate, Arcady Gaydamak, in which numerous French and Angolan officials allegedly received pay-offs and gifts worth US$56 million. The indictment included charges of illegal arms sales, tax evasion, and money laundering. The scandal was tagged 'Angolagate' after 42 prominent people in French politics were indicted, including Jean-Christophe Mitterrand, the son of former President Mitterrand.

Then the London High Court of Justice was given a glimpse into the opaque world of Angolan diamonds in 2012. The same Arcady Gaydamak took his partner, Lev Leviev, a diamond magnate and possibly the largest operator in the diamond industry, to court. Gaydamak sued Leviev for half the assets of the venture – worth a cool £640 million - on the basis of what he claimed was an agreement written and signed in Tel Aviv in December 2001 to share profits from the venture. He also took legal action against Russia's Chief Rabbi, who was said to have been entrusted with the agreement for safekeeping.[55]

What was also clear to anyone who had ever doubted it was that senior Angolan politicians were in the driving seat, accruing massive profits in the diamond industry. Foreigners, no matter how wealthy or influential, had to go through the dos Santos family. During the trial, the involvement of key figures emerged, including Angolan

General Kopelipa, who was thought to hold a position analogous to Prime Minister, an Angolan businessman, and the Chief Executive Officer of Endiama, the state-owned company which issues export licences.

The Court laid bare the opacity of the flow of profits made by Ascorp, the company set up by Angolan President Eduardo dos Santos in 2000 with exclusive rights to buy Angolan diamonds, and raised questions over the role played by Isabel dos Santos, the President's very influential daughter who was at one point the richest woman in Africa. She was extremely good at playing a key role in all major deals. An article by Kerry Dolan in Forbes magazine in 2013 ran with the title '"Daddy's Girl: How An African 'Princess' Banked $3 Billion In A Country Living On $2 A Day".

Andy and I were in full agreement over his assessment of Isabel and her father. He said "Angola was a member of OPEC, it had diamonds, a small population, arable land – it had everything. But nothing filters down in Angola. The President's daughter, Isabel dos Santos, had been educated at Oxford, and she was presumably intelligent. She could have said to her dad, look we've got properties here, in Portugal, in Brazil, and we have plenty of money. Let's leave a legacy. Because the first thing that will happen is the person you leave behind who you schooled to be president will come after you for the money. How much would it have cost to do some good stuff - housing, solar power - so people could have ended up loving him?"

Sure enough, in January 2024, Angolan prosecutors charged Isabel dos Santos with 12 crimes, accusing her of causing state losses of around $219 million while she was head of state-owned oil company Sonangol. In October 2024, she lost an appeal to overturn a $733-million global freeze on her assets as part of a lawsuit in London's High Court. A judge granted the asset freeze nearly a year after dos Santos was sued by Angolan telecommunications operator Unitel over loans made while she was on the Board of Directors of a company she controlled in the Netherlands, Unitel International Holdings.[56]

Having worked in many countries in Africa, my friend Maurice who had spent time advising the Angolan oil company Sonangol said "Angola was an interesting and difficult place to work. The Angolans were most capable. They demonstrated killer instincts in their powers of negotiation. They knew what they wanted and they got it."

Bob is still working in Angola all these years later. He says "I hated it for 20 years, but then I realised it was me not them. You can't hate everyone, and we are all responsible. I'm really comfortable. Every weekend I'm out with friends for lunch. You can enjoy it, but you have to learn to temper yourself."

Chapter 13: Independent evaluations are rarely independent

"Not everything that counts can be counted, and not everything that can be counted counts." (attributed to Einstein)

When it was announced in early March 2025 that Elon Musk was going to close down the entire US aid establishment, USAID, Andy commented predictably "Quite right too, they need to take a sledgehammer to it."

"A sledgehammer will do a huge amount of damage. Plenty of life-saving projects will suddenly be axed. Lots of people will lose jobs and this will have a huge knock on effect." I responded, equally predictably.

"Well the ones that do good have to prove their value. For instance, they need to say the number of schools or hospitals that have been built or vaccinations given," he rejoined.

"Look, there's plenty of measurement of aid projects. But just as there are several ways to skin a cat, so there are plenty of ways to measure results. The bigger questions are: are the results massaged by interested parties? Have they had unintended consequences such as increasing corruption? It's complicated. There should be radical reform of the aid organisations, but I don't agree with taking an axe to them," I replied.

"Reform will never happen. But I can agree that the agencies should carry on as long as you get work and bring money home, my love."

"That's mighty generous of you! I must admit, it really fires me up to set off for yet another country to do something entirely useless. Anyhow, I thought you said you got a better return from putting me out on the streets to earn a living – my love?" I say sweetly.

For a moment I mull over the irony that my early enthusiasm about measuring results was one of the arguments I used to put to Andy in support of aid projects. Now he was parroting it back at me while I had moved on in my thinking.

I had became more jaundiced as I saw evaluations fall far short of their claim to independence, and the measurement part become monitoring and learning – and spin. My entrée into independent evaluations left me with an early sense of doubt about how much donor agencies really want to hear blunt criticism, though for many years I believed or maybe hoped that I was wrong.

Early on in my working life, in 1998-99, I was involved in an in-depth evaluation of a UN agency called the UN Capital Development Fund (UNCDF), which was to launch the company carrying out the evaluation as an international leader in monitoring and evaluation. The fund used to finance infrastructure projects, but this had become "old-fashioned development thinking". Fearing that they might become obsolete, UNCDF had said to its funders, mainly Scandinavian and the Dutch government "We are going to transform ourselves into a specialist agency in governance. Evaluate us in three years' time, and if you don't like what you see close us down." The idea of allowing themselves, a UN agency, to be closed down was obviously anathema so the stakes were high. We realised later that UNCDF had spent those three years carefully preparing for our evaluation so that they would not be found wanting.

Our evaluation team started in The Hague, where we were briefed by the donors, then New York for a month of data gathering and interviewing UNCDF staff, several months in about eight countries where they had new governance programmes, then debriefing to UNCDF and the donors. In all, this took 18 months, with several reports peppering our progress.

The team had two very experienced directors in addition to me (very junior) and another person. The month spent in New York was intense, and I felt I was veering out of my depth. The directors realised early on that all conversations we had with every member of staff were being monitored and reported back to the boss. Everyone sang from the same hymn sheet. There were no querying or dissenting voices.

I worked every single day of that month, just taking a half-day off to go shopping, but was so stressed when I didn't find a single shop within a few blocks of my accommodation (I had just set off blindly in a direction), that I gave up and went back to work. I wonder how many other women have spent a month in New York and failed to find a shop!

I went to review UNCDF projects in Mali and Mozambique, where the company had found good local consultants to work with. In Mali, we went to two locations, one of which was legendary Timbuktu. Busy as we were in our three days there, I managed a quick ride on a camel to the despair and perplexity of the camel driver, a swarthy Malian wearing a vivid cobalt-coloured turban, who remonstrated with me "But, Madam, we can take you into the desert for a full or half-day. Wonderful experience. Provide food and drink, see sand dunes."

"Sorry, I'm working. I only have five minutes, and I want someone to take a photo of me!"

I snagged another five minutes in the Archives, where beautifully quilled writing on tenth-century parchments had been perfectly preserved in the dry climate. These were the religious texts studied by students at a time when Timbuktu was considered the centre of world learning. I visited the World Heritage Site mosque. Strangely, Andy's first wife had also been to Timbuktu. It seemed a badge of marriageability, and given Timbuktu's remoteness I felt I didn't have too much to fear about being usurped by a potential wife number three, especially after Al Shebab occupied the city.

One of my meetings took place in a nearby village, where I spent the first two hours in a cramped room sitting on a dirty mattress talking with the all-male village elders, sipping and discreetly pouring away sickly-sweet tea. This was where the Bella lived, a tribe said to be slaves. The Bella men liked their women fat, so the women were obliged to stay indoors as they were fattened up like geese in preparation for foie gras. I met some women sprawled on rugs across the floor and tried to ask a few questions, but soon gave up because it was clear they couldn't understand me even in translation.

The problem with this Mali project was that it had been designed but was not yet underway, so I could only talk with people about what it was meant to achieve, and at best only assess if the conditions seemed right for it to have some degree of success. For instance, were the right people - influencers, decision makers, community groups - going to be involved? But there was nothing to evaluate per se.

The trip to Mozambique took me somewhere I hadn't visited before when I had lived there - the architecturally beautiful but hauntingly sad Ilha de Mozambique, from where Africans were shipped in the Arab slave trade. My Mozambican consultant was very savvy about the aid industry. He himself was a teacher, and the leader of a land rights campaign which had spurned donor financing because, he said, he didn't care to follow donor agendas and interests.

He realised immediately that we were being watched closely, and that all our conversations with the young UNCDF officer were being reported back scrupulously to headquarters. After one conversation, I said to him "I suppose you are going to report that back to New York this evening?" He denied it, but much later back in New York we had dinner with a staffer who had resigned, and who told me it had been his sole job to monitor and analyse everything we did or said. He laughed and said "Of course, that means I read with amusement the comment you made, Ann, about the UNCDF staff member reporting back to HQ!"

When the whole team convened in the UK later to compare notes and reports, I was under pressure in my grading of projects especially the Malian one which had not yet begun. The directors said we couldn't give "x" scores, meaning "too early to judge", though this was the right score in my view. Failing that, I decided on a median score just because I couldn't see how anyone could give a high evaluation in the absence of any activity or result to measure.

The directors weighed in on me to give a higher score, and I realised that they were under intense pressure to amend upwards anything less than top scores. Given the determination and careful planning of UNCDF HQ to achieve a good evaluation, they could be made to look as if they hadn't fully appreciated all the facts or done their work properly and rigorously. Perhaps most significantly, low scores could undermine their company's desirability as evaluators, and jeopardise their chance of winning future contracts.

There are perverse incentives and collusion all around for evaluations to score highly, with only a few criticisms tolerated, and even then they are typically couched in impeccably vague and opaque civil service terminology. I learnt this when I worked as a consultant in DFID, where the preponderance of high project scores actually triggered an internal memo on one occasion expressing concern that maybe evaluations were not quite rigorous enough. In practice, two factors were at play. A mid-to-low score of three would trigger a lengthier more intensive review, which would take more of everyone's time. Secondly, low scores might suggest that the advisors had been at fault, for instance by not ensuring a better design or intervening in time to prevent poor project execution, rather than the implementation team failing per se. The pragmatic option was to avoid a three.

I encountered a similar phenomenon when I was on the team to evaluate the Japan Social Development Fund, a $300 million fund which the Japanese had transferred to the World Bank to manage and run. One of the questions we were asked by the Japanese delegation in Washington was to identify factors or characteristics which resulted in more or less successful projects. However, every single project was scored as either 'highly successful' or 'very successful'. If they were all apparently equally successful, it would be impossible to assess which factors resulted in greater or lesser project success.

Again, as with UNCDF, we had to visit and evaluate a dozen or so projects around the world. I went to Benin, the only country in the world with voodoo as its official religion, and where the capital, Cotonou, means 'mouth of the river of death' in a local language. After my experience in Guinea, I was rather wary of visiting Benin, and was glad that it was only for about ten days.

I went there to visit a child protection project a few years after it was completed, an ex-post evaluation. In many respects, this is the best or only way to check whether something is successful and sustainable without outside funding, and it was an eye-opener to waste a few days just trying to find anyone who knew about it either in the World Bank office or among the project's partners. It was a case of out of sight, out of mind, despite the much vaunted commitment among donors to design and run projects which were sustainable. We eventually discovered one building constructed to house rescued children who had been trafficked. The building was abandoned, the only remaining residents were weeds and termites.

The importance of monitoring and evaluation in aid programmes grew with the Paris Declaration on Aid Effectiveness in 2005, a commitment to improve the quality of aid and its impact on development. This was to be done through better measurement of results in addition to other pledges.

The growing commitment to measure results in international development grafted well onto new thinking in the UK and other developed countries about measuring results of public policy and programmes. It was all part of what was called "New Public Management". This approach reached its heyday under Prime Minister Tony Blair and Chancellor Gordon Brown. Budgets for public services were increasingly allocated on the basis of targets set and achieved.

Targets provided a convenient way to measure and communicate government performance, with all parties happy to collude over successes since political economy theory suggests that organisations and institutions find ways to work around any system – also called gaming.

Crucially, these targets obfuscate the bigger questions about real results or longer-term impact that take much more time to assess, which is hardly helpful for the increasingly media-savvy politicians. Real results such as a reduction in infant or maternal mortality and higher grades in examinations may only happen outside a politician's term in office.

DFID itself proved to be an expert in setting attainable targets, and scored very easily during a government capability review around 2007. It practised isomorphic mimicry par excellence, becoming brilliant at setting targets it knew it could achieve although the average person not working in the aid industry would have been happily unaware of this.

The following year, I happened to work with a young Swedish woman who had carried out some of those UK government capability reviews, including the DFID one. She was amazed and appalled at how poorly the DFID country office staff interacted with those of us working on projects. Our feeling was that they viewed us contractors as too unimportant to meet. As far as we knew, the key advisor supervising our programme never left his office. Attempts to meet him were usually put off, even when we encountered challenges in our engagement with ministry personnel, which was when we really needed him to step in to defend the boundaries of our work.

With the huge increase in funding for DFID, monitoring and evaluation of aid projects and programmes gradually spawned an industry in itself. When I first worked on DFID projects, reviews and evaluations used to be decidedly lower-key, but fairly rigorous. To my mind, there was more of a learning culture in which everyone concerned wanted to know the possible reasons behind any poor results in order to improve. And there was no corresponding fear of the consequences of a poor review, such as money or reputations at stake.

Evaluations in some agencies at the time were possibly too relaxed, as I realised when I discovered that evaluation teams of United Nations development projects in Mozambique did not necessarily travel to project sites, but simply read the reports while sitting around in the capital Maputo, enjoying the restaurants, beaches, and night life. There were some places no one visited, because the mosquitoes were said to be the size of a small fist and far too dangerous. Fully immersed as I was in the Italian aid group when I lived in Mozambique in the early 1990s, I knew that no one ever visited any projects in the city, Chimoio, because in Italian 'ci muoio' (same pronunciation as Chimoio) means "I die here".

As more money was spent on projects in DFID, evaluations became more rigorous, backed up by tools and methodologies, using graphs and statistics, and giving the appearance of quasi-scientific studies. By the time I finished working on DFID projects, most of the large spending programmes had an independently tendered monitoring and evaluation project running alongside the actual implementing project. These parallel projects added the letter 'L', and became the Monitoring, Evaluation and Learning (MEL) projects.

To feed the MEL projects, the implementing projects had to ensure they kept a detailed list of anything and everything that could be measured. The large Nigerian programme I eventually stopped working on, PERL, used to run a week long "learning event" with all its partners once every four to six weeks. Given how little this programme actually seemed to be achieving as far as I could see, people were spending more time learning than doing. Nevertheless, that programme scored A or A+ for each of its eight annual reviews, a perfect example of successful spin in my view.

An independent watchdog was set up in 2011, the Independent Commission on Aid Impact, which reported directly to Parliament. Its remit was to provide independent evaluation and scrutiny of the impact and value for money of all UK government overseas development assistance. I have read a number of the Commission's reports but rarely come across serious criticism or recommendation to close down certain types of projects or change ways of delivering aid.

In the days when country programme evaluations were still being carried out, I worked on two, in Zambia and the Democratic Republic of the Congo, which included everything they had funded over a five-year period. Our evaluation teams met many of the project beneficiaries across the spectrum of projects. However, by the time I did these evaluations in 2007 and 2008, DFID had already introduced its supersonic management information system, QUEST, which meant that it was very difficult or even impossible to access many project documents. You had to ask someone to get hold of specific documents such as project descriptions and evaluations, but you could not be sure of getting your hands on more critical or confidential documents which might have been held back.

We discovered in Zambia that there had been a scandal over a DFID advisor getting personally involved in tendering for the privatisation of the copper mines, only to leave DFID later and join the winning mining company. This reminded me of what DFID had done in Sierra Leone: interfering in mining contracts. We were asked by the DFID country manager to leave this incident out our evaluation report.

One of the things that struck me most over the Zambia review took place during a discussion with several Zambian senior government staff. Asked which of the various projects and support they had most appreciated, the answer was a small project which supported their revenue authority. The reason was that it had enabled them to increase the amount of revenue they collected, which made them less dependent on foreign aid.

A few years later in 2018, having become somewhat wiser to evaluations, I led a team to evaluate a project in Rwanda funded by both DFID and the Swedish aid agency. My colleagues had already worked on the previous year's review, so between the three of us, we knew the project and the country context very well.

We were contracted by a Hungarian company, which was subcontracted by Ernst & Young (EY). Therein lies yet another example of the complexity of contracting and subcontracting arrangements. EY, which specialise in assurance, consulting, law, strategy, tax, and transactions, are hardly experts in international development. I am not sure how far a Hungarian consulting company understood how DFID operated in Africa, and charming though the staff there were, they never provided much useful insight or backup; they simply handled the sub-contracts with me and two others.

The DFID advisor responsible for this project was a Rwandan, who had acquired a reputation for being a little difficult. Essentially, this advisor had decided what the overall score should be for the project, and he expected us to come up with findings to validate his position. On the other hand, the view of the Swedish project manager was that we should of course do an independent evaluation.

We set off to interview a wide range of people in the capital, Kigali, and in other parts of the country. Despite my scepticism that projects can work well in Rwanda without being hijacked by elite interests, the whole team was impressed by the progress made. At the end of our visit, we gave a presentation of our findings and recommendations to the two donor organisations and the implementers, about 20 to 30 people.

We were roundly congratulated on our presentation to the group, which included the head of the DFID office, for having done an excellent job. No one challenged our findings and scores. Later, however, when I was writing up my report, we hit a problem with the DFID advisor, who had tracked changes on our report, riding roughshod over many recommendations without giving any valid reason, and reduced the overall project score.

Suddenly, out of the blue, the company informed me by email that our contract had been cancelled, and the discussions between DFID and EY had not ended in our favour. Our contract was being terminated on the grounds of poor quality of work and lack of proper integration of the team with the DFID office. The Hungarians wrote "Although we strongly feel that there has been a lack of fair treatment, an interference with independence, and an outright stripping away of our right to remedy issues of dissatisfaction, we will not litigate nor demand arbitration. DFID and EY have cautioned that opting for these could damage our reputation and prolong matters indefinitely."

What I found most chilling was that DFID and EY were cautioning us that if we litigated or demanded arbitration, it could damage our reputation. This was pure and unadulterated blackmail, an abuse of power. I spoke with a colleague and friend, a former partner at Atos Consulting who knew the aid industry inside out, and she said airily "Oh don't worry, these things happen. You get difficult personnel in DFID, and there's nothing you can do. This sort of thing happened to us once, and my team objected and ended up being paid nothing for the whole contract. I suggest you don't object, and it will soon be forgotten and won't affect your reputation."

Reassuring though this was on one level, I was fuming over the contract termination. I even called the Swedish advisor and asked her if she had agreed with the termination and, since she hadn't, if she had any idea what was behind it. She was clearly embarrassed, and just repeated that she appreciated that we had done an excellent job.

Mr P had once said to me: "Some donors require 'independent reviews' of large projects. At least one donor requires the review team to have its initial meeting with the donor, who indicates the grade anticipated. Woe betide any reviewer who attempts to award a grade significantly different to that suggested by the local team managing the project. The reviewer soon learns that future business depends on an acceptable grade being awarded. So much for independent reviews."

I decided that I would wait till I had received payment, and then complain. I wrote a lengthy letter to the Permanent Secretary of DFID, providing evidence that our work and engagement with the DFID Office had been exemplary. There was a response and a review was conducted. It took nearly a year to report back to me. There was some question over the quality of our work but without any counter challenge to my evidence. Management and communications procedures within the DFID Rwanda office were considered not as strong as they should have been. It was a classic piece of wishy-washy fluff. I am not sure I ever thought I would receive serious redress, but in any case it gives me a little satisfaction that I rattled their cage, albeit briefly.

Shortly after this, in 2019-20, I was invited to be part of the evaluation team conducting annual reviews of another major programme funded by many agencies including DFID. It was providing support to trade to the five member countries in the East Africa Community. The project was called Trade Mark East Africa.

The official reviews and evaluation company which subcontracted me for this programme was a Swedish one, and the first year went reasonably well, though I raised a number of challenges. The second year coincided with Covid. I was given the task of reviewing the programme in Uganda. Here I had an advantage because although I could not visit the country, I was in contact with a British relative who is not only an expert agricultural economist (and most trade in Uganda revolves around agriculture), but had lived in Uganda for over 20 years. He is so experienced and knowledgeable that for many years he was brought in by USAID to be their expert, and you can be sure that the Americans would have looked far and wide for an American to fill this post before employing a foreigner.

In addition to wading through about a hundred documents on this project and having 40 or so virtual meetings, my relative gave me other documents he felt were relevant and, finding it an interesting subject, I read further still. Some of these documents provided strong grounds for being fairly critical of the Uganda programme. For instance, one of the planned activities was to build warehouses to store grain, but there was already a surplus of warehouses built by many donors over the years. Many stood empty, and some were used by local communities for sports such as table tennis.

By raising criticisms once again, I came up against the full weight of resistance from all concerned in the Trade Mark East Africa management team and the Swedish consultancy agency. Interestingly though, I had one short email from a DFID Advisor saying "Keep probing, you are asking the right questions." But after lengthy emails and exchanges, the programme team would not accept most of my arguments, and awarded themselves an overall A grade, overriding my B grade.

If nothing else, independence has flown out of the window. Needless to say, I was not invited to be part of the next annual review, and it was at that point that I decided to stop working in the aid business.

Final Chapter: Adaptation and decline

Twenty years ago, Andy and I came to live in South-West France. Not to be confused with glamorous South France, the South-West is very rural and unspoilt, home to more ducks and geese than people. In the twentieth century, the main immigrants were Italians departing from the poverty of northern Italy and Spanish people fleeing the Spanish civil war. They integrated well, quickly adopting the French language and local dialect. The British arrived later and generally we haven't integrate as well but are welcomed kindly nevertheless.

We knew we had been properly accepted once local people started joking with us, coming up with all the stereotypes and long historical rivalries between the French and the English. Our adaptation to this new place was helped in particular by our neighbour, Denise, who came by the house to meet us on day one and advised us on all manner of things such as laws, customs and where to buy the best wine. She was born in the house opposite ours and had been secretary to the local mayor for many years. This meant that she knew everything about everyone, which probably did not endear her to many neighbours and maybe explains why she embraced foreigners.

The house we bought had a pond with four ducks, but the numbers had got whittled down to one by the time we spent our first week there. Denise offered to feed the last duck while we were away working.

The second time we stayed at the house coincided with an alert over avian flu and the French Government issued a decree which set out an obligation to all duck owners to confine so-called domesticated ducks in an enclosure. Failure to do so would result in a fine of E300. Although we felt it would be difficult in practice to enforce this decree with so many ducks around, if anyone was going to be fined we were sure it would be the newly arrived foreigners.

Someone told us he would take the duck off our hands but we must first catch it. We thought this should be an easy task, given the duck had up till then never indicated a proclivity for flight. However, the duck suddenly realised that it did indeed know how to fly and we failed to catch it. We were on our last day before flying back to England. Time was running out. While I was mulling over what to do, Andy took action. He loaded his air rifle and shot the duck. End of story. Or so we thought.

A few months later, I flew back to France ahead of Andy. Denise came by, very sorry to tell me that she had seen no sign of the duck. I had to decide quickly if I should agree with her that perhaps a fox had got the duck – which I would have preferred to do – or to tell her the truth. Knowing that Andy would have no qualms about recounting his story of shooting the duck, I realised the fox story wouldn't wash. She looked mightily displeased and went off in a huff. When Andy arrived, she came to the house and announced that since he was so keen to follow "every silly little French law" – even one due to come into effect on 'poisson d'avril' (April Fool's Day) – he would surely like to know about the latest one. All foreigners whose wives were above a certain height were obliged to shorten them by cutting them off at the head or ankles. Having delivered this announcement in her most serious voice, she then relented and we all laughed. "Stay for lunch" Andy said "we're having duck".

Fast forward 20 years and we are now fully involved in our local community. We have retired and my 'swashbuckling' husband - to quote Maurice - is typically dressed in his post-diamond gear: shorts with holes and ripped pockets, a filthy T-shirt which may originally have been white, and steel toe cap boots. Today he is off with his chainsaw and axe to chop firewood for an elderly English friend.

"This is the only thing that gives me a sense of purpose," he jokes with just a touch of truth, but his new job description encompasses many activities small and large that fall into the "helping neighbours" category, and chopping wood is only one. Calling friends who live alone to jolly them along is another, and passing on any manner of information about plumbers, electricians, clockmakers, water diviners and dentists a third.

I ask him to pick up bread and drop in on Denise, now a frailer 94 years old. She is still a fighting force mentally, and she calls Andy her bête noire. He is one of the few people who can get away with tweaking her ear, teasing her, and bullying her into drinking more water. At times, when she has had periods of extreme weakness and exhaustion, he ramps up the bossing. He orders her to get out of her nightgown and get dressed, and stands over her until she drinks a glass of water. If she continues to look frail, he announces that he is going to move in with her.

"Which side of the bed should I sleep on?" has the rather speedy effect of bringing Denise out of her stupor. A spark of defiance, which morphs into outrage, flares in her face. She creaks a quiet "non", clears her throat, and works up to a "NON". We giggle, and she joins in, smiling determinedly. It is theatre which has been repeated often and ensures she returns to her more usual combative self.

"How are you going to finish your book?" Andy asks.

"Our book," I mutter peevishly and dishonestly, because really I have been the driver and have dragged Andy along on a venture he has been doubtful about throughout the year.

The sociologist in me says a few fine stories doth not a theory make. A colleague of mine from Burundi, Firmin Sindaye, remarked recently that after 70 years or so of independence, it must be said that aid has not achieved its intended objectives given most sub-Saharan African countries remain poor. The massive sums dispensed in aid and the poor and worsening social conditions (health, education, etc.) suggest that aid does not work and it probably exacerbates corruption. But does one really cause the other or are there other explanatory factors at play? We need to join the dots. A causal explanation is obviously intricate, given we are talking about 54 countries, or the variously defined 46 or 48 countries in Sub-Saharan Africa.

On the basis of the stories and examples in this book and my own experience, I believe that the various dysfunctionalities and disincentives within the aid system are largely to blame for the failure of aid to deliver better results. Both sides – donors and recipients – are responsible for playing along with this dysfunctional system.

What I have learnt is that it is generally the small projects and the small aid programmes in specific countries which have added the most value and had the most impact. The large programmes with dozens or more companies in consortia require a lot of public relations to mask their paltry achievements. The so-called independent evaluations are rarely independent, and anyhow they only evaluate the immediate results of the individual projects rather than looking at the bigger picture. The industry of monitoring, evaluation, and learning is sadly mired in the same obfuscation as the projects it monitors. It is like today's customer services which rarely satisfy the customer.

As I was finishing this book, the shock announcement that USAID was to be closed in March 2025 came just after the UK announced that aid would be dropped from 0.5 per cent to 0.3 per cent of gross national income from 2027 onwards. The 0.3 percentage is no lower than it was in 1999, but it probably amounts to less money in real terms given the broader goals of UK aid now include support to refugees entering the UK.

Fortunately, no one stooped to calling UK Aid a criminal organisation or a viper's nest of radical-left Marxists. Instead, the more measured reason given for the budget reduction was the need to increase the UK's spending on defence, as has been the case across Europe. This is in response to America's insistence that we should defend ourselves rather than relying upon our old ally. Other European countries - the Netherlands, Belgium, France, Switzerland, Germany and Sweden - have just cut or announced they will be cutting their international aid budgets due to political and economic pressures.[57]

There is a real sense that international aid is in a state of crisis in a dramatically changing world order. And international aid has overplayed its hand. As budgets increased exponentially in the last two decades, its profile rose, and more criticism has been directed at aid agencies, consultancy companies, and in some cases NGOs. It seems to be in freefall decline.

The Financial Times correspondent for Africa, David Pilling, wrote an excellent summary of the changes in the history of aid, the perspectives of those both for and against it, and the likely future trends. As he said "predicting the probable impact of aid withdrawal depends on your assessment of how good it was in the first place."[58]

In addition to "saving lives", another major argument in favour of aid is the fear of what will happen as western influence in the global south is weakened. However, the soft power of China has been growing in Africa over the last two decades despite the massive aid spending by the West in that same period. I suspect that the influence and soft power argument is precisely a concern of the West and not of the Global South itself. And Firmin Sindaye confirmed my view when he wrote to me "There is a perception that development aid is a tool of the superpowers to maintain pressure on governments in the South, particularly in sub-Saharan Africa, to keep them subservient."

Pilling noted with interest that pushback from USAID's closure has been more muted in recipient countries, citing the Director General of the World Trade Organisation, Ngozi Okonjo-Iweala, saying "In Africa, we really need to change our mindset. Access to aid? I think we can really begin to think of it as a thing of the past."

There are other examples. Speaking at the opening of the African Causus meeting of the World Bank and International Monetary Fund in Ghana in 2019, the Ghanaian President, Nana Addo Dankwa Akufo-Addo said Africa's "Transformation Beyond Aid" was essential and "Africa is eager, Africa is willing."[59] Since Trump's order to freeze foreign aid, there are some signs that African governments are stepping up to fill the gap in financing. Nigerian lawmakers approved an additional $200 million for the health sector and the South African government announced plans to fill the gaps in funding for HIV/AIDS.[60]

Pilling concluded that altruism is not dead, but there will be more self-interest in development plans. The US initiative to build a railway linking mines in Zambia and the Democratic Republic of Congo with a port on the Atlantic coast of Angola is an example of a strategic interest for the United States, which seeks to counter China's grip on critical minerals in the continent.

I take the European view that it is better to reduce aid budgets substantially and wind down large aid projects rather than take the draconian option of closing down a major aid agency. A lot of Africans and foreigners are employed in the many aid agencies and on aid projects. Even if their employment is not in itself the intended goal of these projects, losing jobs will have an impact on people's lives until they find new means of support.

And the slogan "Trade not Aid" launched back in 1964 – emphasising the promotion of free trade of African exports rather than giving aid - needs to be taken off the shelf and dusted off. Fairer international trade along with promoting industrialisation, technology transfer and transparency especially in the mining sector are among

Firmin Sindaye's short list of what developed countries could best do for Africa.

The diamond industry is also in decline, with technology and changing tastes and aspirations largely dictating its future. For those who remain convinced that it is a wicked industry mired in conflict and corruption, this may be good news. Lab-grown diamonds are quickly deciding the fate of the genuine article – indeed, they too are a genuine article.

A lot of people will lose their jobs here too. In 2023, over 15,000 people were employed in the diamond industry in South Africa, and around 25,000 directly or indirectly in Botswana. Many also work in the other large diamond-producing countries of Angola and the Democratic Republic of the Congo. There will be a knock-on effect for those employed indirectly, providing food, logistics and accommodation on-site, and polishing rough stones in countries such as India and Israel.

In the 2024 elections in Botswana, the ruling party lost power for the first time in nearly 60 years. Despite being one of the best-run countries in Africa, the presidency was rattled by an economic slump and allegations of corruption and mismanagement, and falling demand for diamonds due to competition from synthetic stones had knocked the economy.[61] Sadly, Botswana failed to diversify its economy to reduce its reliance on diamonds, which still account for four-fifths of the country's exports.

It is true that the industry needs to clean up its act further. There are ongoing campaigns to improve the rights of workers, their wages, and working conditions. Mining companies could do more to protect these rights, but the pressures on their costs are considerable and several have gone out of business. If African diamond mining companies were to aspire to the exemplary standards of say companies in Canada, they might not last long.

The problems in Canada are multifaceted. Mining companies there have provided excellent environmental, health and safety regulations and conditions, and additional support to Inuit and Cree communities. However, their costs are very high due to the logistics of transporting spare parts and diesel to the mines along icy roads, and the price of fuel has increased since the war in Ukraine began. Competition from lab-grown stones has reduced the average price from the average mine. With falling prices and increasing costs, at least two mines, Victor and Jericho/Renard closed down in the space of a few years.

Bob put it to me in these words "Lab-grown diamonds are an absolute disaster for the industry, without a shadow of a doubt. The latest generation thinks diamonds are old-fashioned and for their parents. Why would you buy a one-carat polished diamond for an engagement ring costing $11,000 when you can get the same thing to a subatomic level for $1,000? It is the end of the industry apart from the big sizes - we're talking six carats and above in the rough, which corresponds to three carats in polished - which get an IGA certificate. Because rich people will always buy those. They do not want anyone to think they've bought some kind of cheap supermarket jeans instead of Calvin Kleins. All the companies would have to do is to hit the marketing really heavily together – just using a small percentage of their budgets - and say look, this is the real thing, it's been there for three billion years. Or do you want something made in a few days? Or speak of the social side of it: we employ thousands of people and that helps their families too. But it won't happen because everyone leaves it to De Beers to do the marketing."

The question is, can De Beers reinvent themselves with a new marketing slogan or is it game over for natural diamonds?

Industries and employment change over time. The fascinating, challenging and frustrating jobs Andy and I were able to do will soon cease to exist. They obliged us to see the world differently, to appreciate and respect the perspective and attitudes of Africans. I hope and trust that new industries and new employment opportunities will emerge in African states as they are obliged to move away from aid dependency.

Glossary and Acronyms

Alluvial diamonds – are diamonds found along riverbeds rather than underground in open cast or deep mine shafts

Blood diamonds – was the term given to diamonds extracted in conflict countries, particularly Sierra Leone and Angola, where they were said to finance or fuel conflict.

Central Selling Organisation was the previous Diamond Trading Company of De Beers

CSOs – Civil Society Organisations

DAG – Development Assistance Group

DCI – Diamond Counsellor International

DFID – Department for International Development (UK), which later became the FCDO (see below)

Direct and sector budget support – are methods of financing the budget of a beneficiary country through a transfer of funds from a donor agency to the beneficiary national treasury (in the case of direct budget support) or to a government budget which is managed in a national account by a government entity for a specific set of sector or programme results (sector budget support).

Donors and donor agencies – are also called development partners in much literature. These terms refer to organisations (national such as DFID; international such as the World Bank or United Nations) which provide international aid to poorer less developed countries.

DRC – Democratic Republic of Congo

DTC – Diamond Trading Company, part of the De Beers Group

FCDO – Foreign Commonwealth and Development Office (UK)

FEPAR – Federal Public Administration Reform Programme

GDO and GGDO – Government Diamond Office and Government Gold and Diamond Office

GDP – Gross Domestic Product

Global Witness – an NGO with considerable expertise in the extractive industries (oil, minerals, diamonds)

IGA – International Gemological Alliance (a certification scheme for diamond quality and authenticity)
Kimberley Process – the process established by the United Nations, diamond industry, NGOs and other relevant parties to seek to halt the sale of diamonds which are fueling or financing conflict. Its remit was later

extended to cover diamonds sold in countries where there are found to be human rights abuses of the diamond employees or diggers.

NDMC – National Diamond Mining Company, the company which took over from Sierra Leone Selection Trust (SLST)

NGO – Non-governmental organisation. Also described as charities.

ODA – Overseas Development Administration (UK), the UK aid body responsible for the delivery of international aid and humanitarian assistance from 1979 to 1997.

Pan Africanism – is a nationalist movement that aims to encourage and strengthen bonds of solidarity between all indigenous peoples and diasporas of Africa

PERL – Partnership to Engage, Reform and Learn project in Nigeria

QUANGO – Quasi Autonomous Non-Governmental Organisation

SLST – Sierra Leone Selection Trust, one of the diamond mining companies in Sierra Leone

Structural adjustment programmes – were introduced after the debt crisis in the 1980s in the wake of the oil crisis. Several African countries defaulted on their debt, so the International Monetary Fund solution was to help them restructure by lending money to repay what they owed while demanding certain reforms.

UNCDF – United Nations Capital Development Fund

UNDP – United Nations Development Programme

UNICEF – United Nations Children Fund

USAID – United States Aid agency

World Bank – used here as the common name for the International Bank for Reconstruction and Development. The World Bank Group includes this as well as four other agencies: the International Development Association, the International Finance Corporation, the Multilateral Investment Guarantee Agency and the International Centre for the Settlement of Investment Disputes

Notes

Chapter 2. Guinea – Baptism by fire and the World Bank Debt Tables

[1] Ibrahima Baba Kaké, 'Le héros et le tyran', Jeune Afrique, 1987

[2] Lansine Kaba, Guinean Politics: a Critical Historical Overview, The Journal of Modern African Studies, 5, 1, 1977.

[3] Dash, Leon (28 March 1984). "Guinea's Longtime President, Ahmed Sekou Toure, Dies". The Washington Post. Retrieved 28 January 2023.

[4] https://horizon.documentation.ird.fr/exl-doc/pleins_textes/pleins_textes_5/b_fdi_20-21/27459.pdf

[5] Camp Boiro (https://fr.wikipedia.org/wiki/Camp_Boiro#:~:text=Amnesty%20International%20%5Barchive%5D%20estime%20que,de%20Sékou%20Touré%20en%201984)

[6] Révolte des femmes du marché de Conakry, en Guinée (https://perspective.usherbrooke.ca/bilan/servlet/BMEve/1036&langue=fr)

[7] General of the People's Army of Vietnam and later Minister of Defence of the Democratic People's Republic of Vietnam (North Vietnam), Vo Nguyen Giap was regarded as one of the greatest military strategists of the 20th century.

[8] see for instance: https://www.cogneurosociety.org/buildings-beauty-and-the-brain-qa-with-anjan-chatterjee/

[9] Structural adjustment programmes were introduced after the debt crisis in the 1980s in the wake of the oil crisis. Several African countries defaulted on their debt, so the IMF solution was to help them restructure by lending money to repay what they owed and demand certain reforms.

[10] Shakran Vedantam and Bill Moser, 'Useful Delusions: the Power and Paradox of the Self-Deceiving Brain', 2021

[11] Days Of Colonization (https://www.tourhq.com/article/days-of-colonization)

[12] Evacuation due to psychological reasons such as symptoms of terror and crazy behaviour

[13] Diallo has received significant accolades for her work in African education and was named one of the 100 Most Influential Africans in 2013 and 2014. See https://en.wikipedia.org/wiki/Aïcha_Bah_Diallo

Chapter 3: Diamonds in the Wild West of Zaire

[14] https://www.gia.edu/diamond-history-lore

[15] A British expression for someone who lives by his or her wits, negotiating and dealing.

Chapter 5. Landmines and an urban project in Angola

[16] South Africa among other nations had supported the UNITA rebel forces fighting the Angolan MPLA government, which was supported by Soviet and Cuban forces and therefore on the "wrong side" of the Cold War

[17] The full British expression is: 'finders keepers, losers weepers' meaning he or she who finds something is entitled to keep it; it's hard luck to the owner.

Chapter 7. The dupes of darling Rwanda

[18] Philip Gourevitch, We Wish to Inform You That Tomorrow We Will Be Killed With Our Families: Stories from Rwanda, 1998, Picador
[19] BBC, 1 May 2024, 'Key Mining Town seized – DR Congo rebels', report by Samba Cyuzuzo
[20] Michela Wrong, Do Not Disturb: The Story of a Political Murder and an African Regime Gone Bad, 4th Estate Harper Collins, 2021
[21] The Guardian, 22 November 2006
[22] Relations were subsequently restored, and France carried out its own investigation which played down her role in the genocide.

[23] Philip Gourevitch, We Wish to Inform You That Tomorrow We Will Be Killed with Our Families: Stories from Rwanda, 1998, Picador
[24] Michela Wrong, op cit
[25] The volcanic range which spans Rwanda, Uganda and the Democratic Republic of the Congo is home to the endangered silverback mountain gorilla.
[26] A minority ethnic group in Kenya and Tanzania.
[27] Sjors Overman, 2016, 'Autonomous Agencies, Happy Citizens? Challenging the satisfaction claim', Governance: an International Journal of Policy, Administration and Institutions, 25 April.

Chapter 8. Diamond poacher turned gamekeeper – the story of Martyn Marriott

[28] Tony Hodges, 'Angola from Afro-Stalinism to Petro-Diamond Capitalism', 2001, The International African Institute's African Issues, James Currey
[29] Dambisa Moyo, Dead Aid: Why aid is not working and how there is another way for Africa, 2009, Penguin Books
[30] Financial Times article, 'Could T-shirts be the way to industrialise an African nation?' David Pilling, 29 August 2024 (data source: IMF Conference Board, the Maddison Project)
[31] Founded in 1827, Fourah Bay could be considered the second oldest if the religious scholastic college of Timbuktu, based on the teaching in three mosques in the 11th and 12th centuries in Mali, is taken into account.

[32] https://www.globalwitness.org/en/blog/are-winds-change-blowing-through-diamond-sector
[33] Chaim Even-Zohar, Diamond industry strategies to combat money laundering and the financing of terrorism, ABN-AMRO, Belgium, 2004

Chapter 9. Nigeria – rats, bats and The Aid Show

[34] House of Commons Library Briefing Paper Number 7996, 4 May 2020
[35] Adam Tooze, Rich countries tilt the scales when it comes to aid, Financial Times, 30 August 2024
[36] William Easterly, The White Man's Burden: Why the West's Efforts to Aid the Rest Have Done So Much Ill and So Little Good, Oxford University Press, 2006
[37] Dambisa Moyo, Dead Aid: Why aid is not working and how there is another way for Africa, Penguin, 2009
[38] Nicola Banks and Dan Brockington, Mapping the UK's development NGOs, The University of Manchester Global Development Institute, Working Paper Series 2019-035, January 2019
https://hummedia.manchester.ac.uk/institutes/gdi/publications/workingpapers/GDI/GDI-working-paper-2019035-banks-brockington.pdf
[39] Multilateral agencies are cross-country, such as United Nations agencies (of which UNICEF is best known) and the World Bank, as opposed to bilateral agencies such as the British or French aid bodies.
[40] Edward Clay, UK High Commissioner to Kenya

[41] https://lordslibrary.parliament.uk/uk-aid-spending-statistics-and-recent-developments
[42] https://en.wikipedia.org/wiki/Economy_of_Nigeria
[43] Sam Unom, founder of Spade Consulting, and the Harvard Africa Policy Journal "Africa's Economic Development is Impeded by Irregular Legacy Institutions: A Rejoinder to Jorge C. Cardoso" 4 January 2019
[44] Financial Times interview of Aanu Adeoye with Nigerian entrepreneur Tony Elumelu 'America was colonised too and look where they are', 9 August 2024
[45] Pritchett, Woolcock and Andrews, Capability Traps? The Mechanisms of Persistent Implementation Failure, Centre for Global Development, Working Paper 234, 2010
[46] Information obtained on the UK Government Development Tracker.
[47] The first one built in Nigeria started production in 2023.

Chapter 11. Ethiopia and tales of NGOs

[48] Michela Wrong, I Didn't Do It For You: How The World Used and Abused a Small African Nation, Harper Perennial, 2005
[49] Nicola Banks and Dan Brockington, Mapping the UK's development NGOs, The University of Manchester Global Development Institute, Working Paper Series 2019-035, January 2019.

[50] Patrick Chabal and Jean-Pascal Daloz, Africa Works: Disorder as Political Instrument, African Issues, The International African Institute with James Currey and Indiana University Press, 1999.
[51] Daniel Jordan Smith, 'Corruption, NGOs and Development in Nigeria', Third World Q. 2010; 31(2): 10.1080/01436591003711975.
[52] https://acso.gov.et/en (viewed in October 2024)

Chapter 12. Daring deeds and scandal in Angola

[53] A British colloquial expression meaning absolutely nothing
[54] 'it's our turn to eat' is a saying used by communities and political leaders especially in Kenya when their party wins an election, after having been excluded from the rich pickings and spoils from the last political party in power
[55] Reuters 15 June 2012, The Jerusalem Post 2 July 2012, RAPSI Russian Legal Information Agency 16 April 2014, Database of Press Releases related to Africa APO Source 29 June 2012
[56] https://www.icij.org/inside-icij/2024/10/angolas-isabel-dos-santos-loses-appeal-to-overturn-global-asset-freeze/

Final chapter: Adaptation and decline

[57] 'Utterly devastating': Global health groups left reeling as European countries slash foreign aid (https://www.euronews.com/health/2025/03/07/utterly-devastating-global-health-groups-left-reeling-as-european-countries-slash-foreign-)

[58] David Pilling, Can international aid survive in a crumbling world order?, Financial Times, 4 March 2025

[59] Africa's transformation Beyond Aid is a must - President (https://mofep.gov.gh/news-and-events/2019-08-02/africas-transformation-beyond-aid-is-a-must-president)

[60] Beyond dependency: Rethinking Africa's relationship with foreign aid (https://speakingofmedicine.plos.org/2025/03/21/beyond-dependency-rethinking-africas-relationship-with-foreign-aid/)

[61] David Pilling, Joseph Cotterill and Rob Rose, 'Diamond-rich Botswana's ruling party loses power after 6 decades', Financial Times, 1 November 2024

Acknowledgements

First and foremost, I thank Andy for all his love and support which has always come with a healthy dose of teasing, joking, encouragement and negotiation during the wonderful 20 years we have spent together so far. I appreciate his agreeing to be bullied into contributing details about buying and advising on diamond valuation.

A huge thanks to Anna-Marie Ball, Bill Fraser and Maurice Fitzgerald for reading early and later drafts and giving advice and pointers to improve the book, especially dear Anna-Marie who kindly read both the earlier and later versions of the document and gave a lot of invaluable technical and general feedback.

Some of their feedback included questions such as whether this was really one book or two, one on diamonds and one on aid? I felt it was more interesting to include the two together and I don't think I had enough material for either by themselves. Two readers felt I should make more of the love story leitmotif which runs through and binds the two stories but I felt a little goes a long way and it's not really my thing to write about my personal life in detail. It is perhaps for these reasons that literary agents chose to steer a wide course from it or maybe the pressure they are under to only take on known and successful published writers meant I was never going to get a foot through a door. I will admit that I was also rather lazy about trying to engage them and publishers directly because I am impatient and wanted to get my book out immediately while the subjects of aid and diamonds are in the news frequently.

Thanks to Clare Wadsworth for editing the book and giving advice for making improvements, in addition to sending me articles of interest on the subjects in the book.

Thanks to Tom Greenhill for helping me go down the route of self publishing through to design of the book cover. It may be described as easy but a young IT expert can appreciate the so-called ease better than a retired aid worker of my ilk.

I want to thank various individuals who kindly contributed their thoughts and views on these subjects. On diamonds, my heartfelt appreciation goes to Martyn Marriott who provided me with lengthy detail about how he helped transform the diamond industry in Botswana. His accounts of his company's dealings in Sierra Leone and Angola were also essential. Martyn's soul is and always has been very much pro-African and over the years of meeting him and hearing about him, I felt sure I could rely on his perspectives without reservation. The friend who played matchmaker (no doubt unwittingly) between Andy and me, Bob Gollifer, also has what I consider a balanced perspective on the industry. His father worked in agriculture in the aid industry and I suspect influenced his views about respecting rather than exploiting Africans.

On aid, many thanks to a number of Europeans who contributed accounts of their experiences in the industry, especially Bill Fraser, the elusive Mr P, Mary Daly and Gil Long.

From a wider perspective, I appreciated the accounts of Maurice Fitzgerald whose fascinating and varied career embraced diplomacy, banking and the World Bank, and Bernard Debord, an award winning journalist.

I give the views of a number of Africans and want to thank them for the insight they gave me over the years, including Cherif Diallo, Sam Unom, Firmin Sindaye and John Daramy from (respectively) Guinea, Nigeria, Burundi and Sierra Leone. Shortly after I had finished writing the first draft of this book, John Daramy sadly passed away. He was a close friend of Andy's for more than 30 years and is sorely missed.

Retirement was not an easy experience for me initially but over time it has become a rich one filled with many projects, hobbies and my social network. I am about to embark on a second book. Painting remains a passion. Feeling loved and supported by my close circle of family and friends has enabled me to have the confidence to write, so a special thanks to those important people in my life – my nephew Douglas, Andy's sons and their families, our two sisters Sara and Caroline and my Italian family in addition to close friends. A final appreciation for my departed Uncle Ian, from whom I received a generous inheritance which I used to bring this manuscript to the point of publication. I hope he would have enjoyed reading it.

France
June 2025

Questions for Book Clubs

1. Does Ann's experience of working in international aid make you more likely or less likely to view international aid as a good or bad thing?

2. What did you consider were the positive and negative stories of aid in this book? Do you have any examples of stories which have shocked you about aid being wasted or fuelling corruption in Africa or elsewhere? Have you heard of very positive stories about aid?

3. What do you think about the Wild West days of the diamond industry? Did you find Andy's early stories in the two Congos amusing or did you disapprove – or indeed both?

4. What did you think about Martyn Marriott's story of helping to transform the diamond industry in Botswana? Why did it prove difficult to do the same thing in other African countries?

5. For both industries, who do you feel is responsible for the positive or negative results? Is it African governments or citizens? Is it foreign governments, aid agencies and all the other players such as NGOs and private companies? Or a combination of all these bodies?

6. What did you think about the relationship between Ann and Andy? Could you see how these different characters could be attracted to each other?

7. Have you or would you buy a mined diamond or a lab grown one? Or would you rather spend your money on something else?

Printed in Dunstable, United Kingdom

64308232R00181